22

WOMEN ULTRAPRENEURS & HISTORY-MAKING COUPLES

Leaving Legacy in Network Marketing

Tell All

22 Women Ultrapreneurs & History-Making Couples Leaving Legacy in Network Marketing Tell All

Copyright © 2022 Mission Accepted Media, Deb Drummond.

For speaking inquiries, permission requests, and bulk order purchase options, www.DebDrummond.com

DEDICATION

We don't get to where we get to in life by ourselves. I want to dedicate this book to those people who have allowed me the grace to be the entrepreneur that I am.

I want to recognize those people I have leaned into for encouragement and support in my entrepreneurial and personal life.

To Lyza Ulrych, Debbie Hawes, and Pete Holt, you have been earth angels in my life. To Tammy Wong, you keep me laughing, to Susan Cameron, you keep me real, and to Rowena List, you keep me loving myself.

I would also like to dedicate this book to those who have given me incredible support in this industry of Network Marketing: Puya Ghandian, Kathy Henken, Angela Martini, and Michael Mulvey.

We know that a project of such importance with many moving parts doesn't happen alone.

Thank you, Jaime Orlow and Shannon Bloschinsky, for your continued support in this project and so many others.

A big-hearted thanks of gratitude to both Dorothea Korthuis and Angel Tuccy, who went ALL IN on all aspects of this project from beginning to end. Multiple meetings and trusted advice made this book the success that it is, thank you so much, ladies.

To my two favourite people …
All that I do and all that I am fills my heart like no other than being the mother to my beautiful daughter Chloae, whose sense of life has always

been graceful, and her level of intelligence leaves me in awe. Her love of books has been there since she could crawl. She would sneak books into bed and read well into the night until she fell asleep. It is such a pleasure to watch her share her love for reading with her own 2 gorgeous children, Brynnlee and Kashton.

As well, my love and gratitude extend to my extremely talented and creative-minded son, Ocean. With his love for music, eye for fashion, talent for art, and desire for entrepreneurship, he reminds me every day to stay cool, stay calm, and just let things unfold.

Thank you for reading this book. I hope this book helps you find your way to becoming a "Gentle To Yourself But Powerful To The World" person in business that brings you to a place beyond your wildest dreams.

Your new friend,
Deb Drummond

Leaving Legacy in Network Marketing

Tell All

TABLE OF CONTENTS

JACK M. ZUFELT

INTERNATIONAL SUCCESS EXPERT AND MLM SPEAKER AND TRAINER

FOREWORD

She has done it again! Deborah Drummond has published another amazing and impactful book about creating success in the Network Marketing industry! This time she features 22 amazing women and couples who share their stories and secrets for success in that industry.

I really like this book because it is chock full of down to earth, very believable stories that will lift and inspire all who read it! It's full of wonderful insights and brilliant concepts that work! It is fun and easy to read it and will be a treasure to you and your organization!

As a highly successful business woman and an award-winning expert herself, Deborah brings a wealth of wisdom and expertise to your world! This is a fabulous resource that can help you create income too. What you will learn from this book could cause you to soar to the top in this industry just like the women and couples featured in this book did!

In a poll of adults 99% said their first concern is family. 98% said financial issues were their number two concern. This huge concern about family and financial matters makes Network Marketing (MLM) a perfect, affordable business to be involved in to take of those two major concerns. And these amazing people show you how *they* did it.

Having been a venture capitalist for many years I raised and invested over $20 million dollars in many business ventures that I owned with the investors. Businesses like two coal mines in Kentucky, computer games, real estate, and 14 franchises. And....I made more net cash flow as a distributor in network marketing than all of those businesses combined. And without the debt and substantial overhead.

It is my observation and personal experience that for just a few dollars out of pocket and the right effort, no other business can generate as much net cash income as a thriving MLM organization. The individuals and couples featured in this book are proof of that!

It's a fact that with a lot of drive and clear direction, anyone can make money in MLM. This book provides the clear direction on how to do that from some of the brightest minds in the world. If you want to be successful, copy people who are already successful.

MLM provides the least expensive, least risky way to generate income that exists today…and you don't need a formal education or previous business or sales experience. All you need is a Core Desire© combined with proper direction (how to's) from successful people. There are 22 great examples in this book.

My best-selling book, The DNA of Success, goes into what it really takes to achieve success….in any area of life. It includes a whole chapter about finding qualified mentors – someone who has successfully done what you want to do.

If making a lot of money is one of your Core Desires© this book not only covers many of the critical points you must know about to make big income in MLM -- it also gives you access to advice and personal direction from some of the greatest minds in the industry. It is rare to see a compilation of highly qualified MLM mentors in one book. This book is a real treasure for all who want to build a successful MLM organization.

As an internationally recognized success expert I can say without hesitation that Deborah has done a wonderful job in putting together this awesome collection of wisdom and experience to share with you and help you grow your business.

It is a fact that achieving the right attitudes and applying proven techniques can generate substantial income in MLM. The women and couples in this book have proven that. Apply what they share on these pages and you can become a successful MLM business builder too. And – be sure to get everyone in your downline to read it too. Read it NOW!

Jack M. Zufelt

"Mentor To Millions"

Author of the #1 best-selling book

The DNA of Success

Now in 16 languages and sold in 50 countries

www.dnaofsuccess.com

INTRODUCTION

Let me tell you about hope!

Reading this book, you're going to see, hear and literally experience hope in all its possibilities.

When I got the idea to create a book for the Network Marketing Profession, I knew deep in my heart why I was given the vision.

Even after all of these years, all of the success stories, all of the numbers, and all of the countries that have had the Network Marketing business model rescue their economy, after all of the families that have experienced true betterment by unique products that are only shared and sold by word of mouth (which is the best way to get a true read on the result of a product), all of the lives of people being able to create a revenue stream around the demands of their lives, all of the freedom this industry has created, the truth is that there are still people who don't understand that network marketing is a true business and life-changing option.

There are still people who have never even heard of Network Marketing, and they're looking for something different in their lives. They want to, or more importantly, need to, make a change and create income for their families, yet they don't have the start-up costs or business experience to start their own business, or even if they do, they don't have the 5 years it'll take to make that kind of investment back. They need something to help them and they need it right now.

There are people that have heard of our industry but don't really understand it. There are people who may have tried direct sales once and never got to where they wanted to go so they think it's like that for everyone and every company and they don't know what to do or how to be in this industry and have success.

I knew in my heart I wanted to create a book that would truly cast a vision for people, not just in this industry, not just for new people in this industry, but for anyone who needed to be reminded of the incredibleness of what is within reach for everyone.

Yes, I said, everyone!

Our profession is an equal opportunity employer like never seen before, with no glass ceilings ever!

I wanted to create a book that would inspire people who have even been in the profession for 5, 10, 20 years or more. I wanted people who have never heard of this industry to know it's truly a legitimate profession! Whether you do it for a few hours a week or it is your full-time career choice, network marketing is a profession that sometimes doesn't get the accolades or consideration it deserves when someone's in need of making a career change or adding an additional revenue stream to their lives.

Most people don't understand the realness of residual money, they think they do but most people have never had it and it doesn't make sense to them.

Many people don't understand the concept of time value in relationship to financial freedom or financial resources.

It is for all those reasons, and then some, that I knew I needed to roll up my sleeves and get this book to market for you to read and learn and pass it on to someone else to read and learn and pass on ... It is deep in my heart to share about this business.

I have seen it over and over again, both the success and the struggle of entrepreneurship on all levels. In traditional business, corporate, and Network Marketing.

Nothing allows you more opportunity for freedom with minimal entry cost as this profession does.

I searched high and higher for these incredible examples of Network Marketing Professionals doing this business for the right reasons and asked them to share their stories, their insights, and their success secrets to help as many people as possible have the same opportunity someone gave them.

This book is something I knew I had to do, it was a vision that turned into a drive for you the reader, for you to understand how you too can have whatever it is you want from our industry. If you're looking for community: you're in the right place.

If you're looking to be in business but don't have all the funds to open your own traditional business: you're in the right place. If you are looking for an extra side gig income for your job, your own business, or you are needing something part-time or want to completely replace your full income: you are in the right place. If you want to stay home with your kids and not miss out on those events and milestones: you are in the right place. If you tried it before and it didn't quite work out: you are in the right place. If you have success in this profession already but don't know if you can go to the next level: you are in the right place.

I think you get my point!

I don't believe in mistakes and there is no mistake you are reading this book today. It's your day and something in this book is going to "land for you". How do I know this? Because I wouldn't have answered the phone at some ridiculous hour of the morning to answer the call from a publishing house (that I thought was someone else) and within minutes, get struck with a clear message that I needed to do an anthology of network marketing professionals to help share the word if I wasn't supposed to. No mistakes.

I think we can see the vision of the future of being able to create for ourselves what our lives look like and the ability to design our own lives in relation to careers is here to stay. The world has changed, and we have become aware of how we can really (with some support and creativity) have it all. We can spend more time with loved ones and build a business and legacy for ourselves in a way that doesn't mean negating the adage of how things have been in the past, it's the power of knowledge of how we can make our life the way we want it to be based on our needs, our own values and mission in life for ourselves and for legacy.

That, my friend, is why this book is on the market. It's a big vision with you in mind.

Thank you for sharing in that vision by reading all these stories and being open to hearing what might be for you, or for someone you know.

Your new (or maybe not so new) friend,

Deb

It is your day and something in this book is going to "land for you".

FAITH GALLATIN

"Be more of who you are!"

FAITH GALLATIN

I snuck in the back door ... and ended up walking the stage! It is kind of crazy what life will hand you. Crazier still can be how you respond to that gift.

Network Marketing was NOT on any list I wanted to engage in. I had seen way too many people chase the dream and end up worse than before. I was NOT EVER going to call every friend and family member I knew at the end of the month and ask for their social security number just so I could sign them up to meet some required sales volume for me.

Well, never say never!

I agreed to try one more product in a weak moment when I was in the middle of a 5-day hospital stay with my daughter – just so I could have a break to go to the cafeteria to get lunch. That product was amazing. But I couldn't afford it at the time. I was working full-time to put groceries on the table for my family – nothing extra in the budget. However, this product could be earned for free by gaining customers and I knew of 100 moms like me that needed it. So, I signed up figuring I'd get a few customers and free product for myself.

Oh, and there was an iPad bonus available to earn in the first 60 days after signing up. My oldest daughter was born with multiple disabilities including severe speech delays which means she is non-verbal. We had found a great app which speaks for people and had it on an iPod, but her motor skills were too challenged to use that tiny screen. She needed an iPad to use the program. At that time, iPads cost about $500 which of course wasn't available on our tight budget. The sign-up fee for the business was $500. I decided to "borrow" $500 from bills that needed to be paid in 30 days for an opportunity to earn an iPad for my daughter along with $500 in commissions – and she'd have an iPad which didn't cost me anything out-of-pocket. I thought it was a breakeven proposal money-wise and a great way to put sweat equity to work to get her an iPad.

I BET ON MYSELF. I stepped out in faith. And it felt good.

And then I had that "Oh s…" moment because I really didn't know if I could do this.

To top it off, God had even bigger plans. Two weeks after I signed up, I was laid off. Within the next month, my daughter was officially diagnosed with epilepsy and her seizures increased to 60 a day. There was no way I could return to a "normal" work schedule for an employer.

So, I made a choice. A DECISION. I had learned lots of new skills in my past through the years – why couldn't I learn how to build this network marketing business? Why NOT me?

It was hard work. I EXPANDED my comfort zone in enormous ways. I started reading personal development books (and still have three going at any one time). I DARED to purchase an unlimited calling plan on my cell phone (they cost a lot more back then) so I wasn't scared to talk as many minutes as I needed to build my business. I got caregiving coverage for my daughter once a month on my "day off" so I could drive 2 hours each way to attend trainings and meet like-minded people.

But the good news was I could do this work while being with both my daughters 24/7. And my commission checks kept growing as I worked the system and talked to people – on my team and in the rest of the world.

I earned my iPad bonus in that first 60 days. My daughter just retired that device after using it to communicate with her world every day for nine years.

Then there was this car bonus available. In the past, I always thought the "car bonus" offered by companies seemed phony because few people earned it, plus what was the big deal with driving a fancy car? Just another dangling carrot to encourage people to buy more product to put in their garages.

Ok, I do like fast, pretty cars, but I was perfectly happy driving my hand-me-down Corolla with 200,000+ miles and a broken gas cap. If the road noise was too loud, we just turned up the volume on the radio. Our "Tin Can" got amazing gas mileage, too.

That's calling SETTLING for something. And that's a mindset.

You see, I earned my "car bonus" two months after I committed to building my business. But I didn't believe it was real. I kept driving my Corolla while waiting to see if the bonus "went away." Three months later my daughter started seizing every three minutes and I put her in my Tin Can to get to the hospital 2 hours away. The staff at the hospital took my keys to valet park my car while I was with her in the ER. An hour later, a young man returned my keys to me and said they had pushed my car to the side of the parking lot because they couldn't start it. I was literally stranded.

Suddenly a "car bonus" for a new car had nothing to do with me driving a pretty car. It meant SECURITY for my girls. Knowing every time I pressed the start button, I could get them wherever they needed to be.

This was when I also started to see my WHY as much bigger than groceries. It is being able to make sure - because of residual income – that my younger daughter can be a sister to my older daughter and not a live-in caregiver. That I can provide for my family in whatever way I choose. And those options are so much bigger than what I had seen to that point in my life.

Ten years later, I'm still driving my pretty "car bonus" car – well, it's my fourth "car bonus" car. When my daughter's wheelchair wouldn't fit in one car, we just traded it in to get one where it would!

I'm still grateful every day when I press that start button.

Of course, there is the feared roller coaster ride in network marketing – but what part of life is not full of ups and downs?

Speaking of roller coasters, I had been working to reach a certain income level (aka rank) and my girls knew I was pursuing it. They watched me work my business from my computer and phone as I really couldn't leave my oldest alone, so I mastered Zoom way before most people knew what it was. It took an extra three months to reach the goal I had set, and I had to do a lot of mindset work to keep myself in the game. But, as much as I wouldn't wish my circumstances on anyone, I had no other choice but to push on and keep building. So, I did.

The night I hit my goal, my second daughter immediately asked, "Can we go to Disneyland now, Mom?" She had been asking for months to go since her friends had gone, and, at that moment, I was able to say "Yes!" Truly amazing to know we could afford to take this trip together!

We piggy-backed our Disneyland trip right after an annual conference in the Anaheim area. At that conference, I walked the stage in recognition of that goal I'd reached.

I made it to the big stage after sneaking in the back door. And if you choose to, you can, too.

Riding roller coasters with my daughters is always incredible. My oldest needs huge sensory input to know she is moving so she starts crying when the ride is done, wanting more of that feeling. Because of her disabilities and the difficulties in getting her on rides, the staff often allows her to stay on and ride again right away. In every single picture she has her hands in the air and her mouth smiling wide open. It doesn't matter if we're going up or down, she is laughing and saying "More, more!"

We need to RIDE our business experience like she rides the coasters. Smile broader, laugh louder, and scream for "more" as we experience all there is in the ride of our lives.

It's all about CHOOSING to be FREE to be YOU. Be more of who you are!

I call myself a Life Alignment Catalyst. My life purpose is to assist other people in every interaction with moving a little quicker in the direction they want to go to reach their God-given potential. I've learned some skills and tactics, but most of all I am growing every day to be the best version of myself. And it's a never-ending journey this side of heaven.

You need to know who you are and build your business true to yourself. Don't try to be someone else. Sure, get ideas from others having success, but you MUST do your business authentically as YOU. Everyone you talk to knows whether you are sincere or just blowing smoke – and they will respond in kind.

My sponsor is an amazing woman, a top leader in this industry for years. I tried to be just like her – and it helped to copy her at first while I learned the business – but I realized I was NOT her. I could NEVER be her. I can only be ME to the fullest extent possible. And when I am me, I attract the people who like me. Those are the people I can work with best, so it is a WIN-WIN all 'round.

Discover who YOU are. Do your business in the style that is most YOU.

Don't worry about anyone else. Comparison is the thief of joy.

Enjoy talking to people. Find out about who THEY really are. Invite them to work with you if they are your kind of peeps.

There are more than enough opportunities to go around. I believe if each one of us finds our God-given purpose and calling, the world will have no lack.

Please find yours and OWN it.

Faith Gallatin is a Life Alignment Catalyst and Chaos Coordinator. With her life experiences as an author, business owner, team leader, and mom, she delights in using her box of certified tools to assist people in quickly breaking through what's stopping them and moving forward into their true potential. Be more of who you are!

CINDY HAFENBRACK

"Network Marketing helps you prepare for impact. It builds a financial wall around your family that no one can penetrate."

CINDY HAFENBRACK

Prepare for Impact

I prayed for something like this to come into my life.

I prayed to God …" Please God, give me something I can do to give my two sons and mother a better life. Give me something I can believe in with a company that has my back. Oh, and don't make it too hard".

When I hit 'submit' and bought my kit, my heart was pounding. I told myself "Cindy you have no choice. You have no other way to give your sons a better life. This is how you are going to change your life. You have to change in order for your life to change. You have watched other people succeed in this industry, you can too. It can be done! "

What I also had heard was that this industry will also prepare you for impact.

There are a few questions I have always liked to ask people:

- Where will you be in five years if you keep doing the same thing and do not change a thing?
- What if the main bread winner in your house lost their job?
- How long could your savings support you?

When the pandemic hit, we all experienced *impact.*

I live in Seattle, and my 92-year-old mother and 62-year-old disabled brother live in New York. In the beginning of the pandemic, my mom had to let my brother's caregiver go. Of course, she couldn't take care of him all by herself, so I flew to New York to help with his caregiving and to help my mom any way I could. We were overly vigilant during the pandemic and we didn't let anyone in the house because we were so worried my mom would catch Covid. During this time my mom fell and hit her head on cement and had a concussion. Thank Goodness I was there so I could take care of both of them. I stayed and helped both of them for 13 months. We were finally able to find a caregiver and I was able to fly back home to Seattle. Two months later, my brother fell on her and she cracked her pelvis. I was on the next plane back to New York to take care of her and help her recover and heal as she was now on bed rest. I stayed in NY another five months to help both my family members and to care for them. Thanks to my Network Marketing business I not only had the time freedom to help my family I also had the resources to pay for some of my brother's medical needs.

The only reason I was able to stop everything and care for my two family members in need was because of my Network Marketing company and the residual income I could depend on coming in every month. Network Marketing made it possible for me to care for my loved ones when they need me. I also want to add that, while I was busy caring for two family members, my business actually grew!

Network Marketing has been a life jacket for me and my family. It helps your family prepare for impact by helping you build a financial wall that no one can break. When you experience the mental peace and financial security of residual income, you want to tell the world about it. The great news is you have the ability to throw other families the same life saver you have. You have the ability to change people's lives in an extraordinary, positive way.

We need to go back 29 years ago when my love for this extraordinary industry of Network Marketing began.

I was sitting at the little gym with my two young sons, Andy age 7 and Matt age 4, and this gal kept smiling at me. I thought to myself, do I know her? We started chatting and she told me she just started a home-based business with a children's book publisher and asked if I wanted to take a look at her catalog. Of course, I said yes.

Then she nonchalantly mentioned that her friend who told her about this company was earning a great monthly income from her home. I thought to myself no way. I mean, I had heard of people making money in home-based businesses, but never anyone I knew or anyone local.

Then my wheels started turning and I thought to myself, hey maybe I could make a little money and buy that $200 bedspread I had my eye on. It was an expensive bedspread, that's why I had to jump into Network Marketing!

I definitely caught the vision of this industry right away. I got so excited about the possibilities and started to imagine what the future could be like if I got serious and kept my eye on the prize.

I kept saying to myself, if that woman can make that income every month, so can I. This is definitely a mindset that has benefited me throughout my Network Marketing career. In fact, when I think of what has benefitted me the most on my journey, it has been mindset, perseverance and gratitude. If I saw someone else succeeding, I felt I could too. I always felt they don't have anything I don't have. I never said the words, "I can't ".

I wanted what I saw other people achieving in this industry. I wanted the time freedom and the financial rewards. Yes, I fell in love with this industry. When I first discovered this industry, I was shocked that something this wonderful existed. Being able to create a beautiful dream life for my family and help others do the same, well it just didn't get any better than this.

I rolled up my sleeves, put on my blinders and I decided I would do something every day in my business to help bring me one step closer to my goals. I can't remember another time in my life when I was this consistent. However, I was so excited of what this industry could do for my life and the lives of others, I simply just set out to go for it and change some lives.

I fell in love with the journey. I fell in love with taking people from not knowing to knowing about my opportunity. I was so elated with what I had in my hot hands I couldn't wait to tell people about it. I had the ability to make a huge difference and impact in other people's lives. Not everyone has the opportunity to accomplish this, but in this industry we do.

Fall in love with your why ... otherwise known as keep your eye on the prize. I joined this industry to give my two boys a better life. This industry gave me hope for a better future and the license to dream again. As a single mom, I wanted to show my two boys I could do anything I set my mind to. I wanted them to be proud of me. I wanted them to see their mom could make a decision, execute it and stay the course.

To help keep me on track and stay motivated, I made a list of twenty dreams and by twenty dreams, I mean twenty things I wanted this industry to pay for. The dreams started out as survival dreams like pay off my credit card and pay off my dentist. My first dream on the list was to buy organic food. With all the dreams I could possibly come up with that was my first dream. I had to laugh. Then the dreams got to be more fun as you went down the list, take the boys to New York for Christmas to see their grandmother, buy my mom a new car, buy my son a new car, go visit my son Andy at College in Singapore, take the whole family to Italy and Spain. I read this list every day. Plus, I taped it to the wall. I also had my two sons tape pictures of their dreams up on the wall. I knew I would work harder on their dreams. I also taped 8 by 10 pictures of their smiling faces up on the wall overlooking my phone and computer.

On days I didn't feel like working, I just looked up at their faces and said to myself, Cindy, keep going, you're doing this for them. I never wanted to look at my two sons in the eyes and say to them, remember that great business mommy started, and I told you what a great life it was going to give us, well I quit.

Nothing was going to stop me from giving my boys a better life and a life of our dreams.

Was I scared, tired and overwhelmed at times? Yes! But I heard acting in spite of fear was courage. I said to myself, Cindy you need to get a grip and have courage. (I do a ton of self-talk) People told me this *wouldn't work* and *don't do it*. However, that just fueled my fire.

A few years ago, my son Matt said to my mom, Grandma are you proud of my mom? My mom said *yes, I am Matt*. Matt said, *yes Grandma, I am too*. What more could I want?

Fall in love with what this industry can do for your life and live your life in gratitude. I have been very blessed in this industry. I wake up every morning with gratitude and joy because of the kind of life this industry has given to me and my family. My mission is to help others achieve what they want and also have a better life.

When I first discovered this industry, I said to myself, Cindy this is the kind of business you have waited your whole life for. This is going to change your life, your children's life, your mother's life and anyone else who wants to lock arms with me and together we can help each other go after our dreams. I have so much gratitude for what this industry has done for my life and I know what it can do for others. In fact, I felt negligent if I didn't tell them about it. And what is the girlfriend code of honor? When you find something you love you tell them about it. Right?!

I am extremely grateful that this industry has given me the time freedom to be with my family when they need me. When my mother needs me, I can drop everything and hop on the next plane to help her. When my son needs me to babysit my grandson for a few days a week I am available! You can't put a price on time freedom.

To sum it all up, here are my tips:

- Fall in love with your journey
- Fall in love with contacting people to enlighten them about your opportunity
- Fall in love with your list of 20 dreams
- Fall in love with your future
- Fall in love with changing lives

One of my success secrets was I would think of the NEGATIVE outcome if I didn't do what I needed to do to build my business. I was more motivated by negative consequences than positive gain. For example, the idea of eviction or not being able to pay bills was more effective than the possibility of a new house or car.

If I saw other people obtain success, I'd tell myself "If they could do it, then I can do it"

One of the ways I still stay motivated in my Network Marketing business is by realizing I have the best opportunity in town! I realize what I have in my hot little hand, and I don't take for granted this blessing. I don't want to squander what I have been given.

I listen daily to motivational speakers, and it has changed my life.

I go to my company's conference every year.

I feel it is my obligation to share what I have found. I believe people are praying for this opportunity every night.

It just so happens that Network Marketing could turn out to be a dream career that is just waiting for you … to serve anything you desire in life to you on a silver platter! You know about Network Marketing now. Dream big. Dream your wildest dreams.

Cindy has been a Network Marketing Professional since 1994. Prior to this industry, Cindy was a registered nurse. Helping people has always been her passion and Cindy found her calling in Network Marketing. Cindy has a huge heart for helping others see the possibilities and go after their dreams. She feels Network Marketing is one of the best vehicles out there to help people accomplish whatever they desire and to have a beautiful life.

Dream big.

Dream your wildest dreams.

MARIA BIANCHI

"Life may take you where you least expect it but always have faith that you are exactly where you are supposed to be."

MARIA BIANCHI

You never know how strong you are until being strong is the only choice you have. This resonated with me 15 years ago when I was widowed at 37 years old, with three kids ages 6, 12, and 13. Until then I lived a normal life. I got married, had a great job, had some kids, went to church … all normal stuff. And then everything changed. Now began the struggle of being an only parent and the stresses of balancing being home with the kids and being at work providing for them. All I knew is I couldn't fail. I couldn't fail my kids and I couldn't fail at work. I had to succeed at both, and it was going to take focus, determination, and very little sleep!

Just as I was getting a hang of things, I got knocked down again. One week after my 40th birthday I found a lump that turned out to be positive for breast cancer. You could imagine my shock, disbelief and anger! How could this be?! That quickly turned into; okay what's my gameplan, time to fight, I got this! *I had cancer but it did not have me!* I ended up having a double mastectomy, 13 rounds of chemo and then four years later a complete hysterectomy. I had no husband, no boobs and no hair, but I was alive and very grateful for that. I didn't know God's master plan, but I trusted Him. I trusted this would not all be for nothing … at least that's what I hoped.

As I returned to work, I realized my story inspired others and provided hope. I was a single mom, I had battled breast cancer, was thrust into the fire of early menopause and somehow managed to raise three amazing kids and have a smile every day. On the outside I seemed like superwoman. However, behind closed doors, I was struggling with health issues no one knew about, I was doing a job I no longer enjoyed, and I was feeling my life had no purpose.

I was 50, depressed, overweight, with poor digestion, struggling with hot flashes, night sweats, low energy and no passion for life since the death of my dear brother Anthony. I was done. I felt defeated. Every time I got knocked down, I got back up, but this time I was done. I prayed about wanting to be reunited with my husband and brother in heaven. I felt my time here on earth was done. I threw in the towel and God threw it right back at me. That towel had network marketing written all over it. He said you're not done. I've got plans for you. Yup, I heard it just like that!

This is when it caught my eye. My friend Kimberly was posting about her product on social media. I saw her post about how it was helping her, and I thought maybe it could help me too. I reached out to her and told her I was interested. Within a couple of weeks, I was feeling better. Within a couple of months, I had lost 20 pounds, my depression had gone away, I was sleeping better, had more energy and I was thinking about my future! I was seeing improvement in my health I hadn't seen in over 10 years. I was sold on this product, and I knew I had to share it with friends. I knew I wasn't alone with the struggles I experienced. I wasn't about to keep this a secret from all the women that are pretending to be okay every day and really aren't. I had done that myself for a long time.

With a new zest for life and a passion to help women, I started sharing about my products with friends and family. For the first time, in a long time, I was excited about what I was doing. You see, I was praying for a change. I wanted a career that had purpose and I could make a difference in the lives of other people. When I said yes to trying these products, I had no idea all the other opportunities I was saying yes to:

An opportunity to feel better

An opportunity to travel more

An opportunity to impact lives

An opportunity to mentor others

An opportunity to challenge myself

An opportunity to have time freedom

An opportunity to make new friends

An opportunity to work from anywhere

An opportunity to become my own boss

An opportunity to dream bigger than ever before

I'm so grateful God put this opportunity in my path! In my first three months I fell in love with the products. In six months, I fell in love with me again. I had lost 40 pounds, felt great, and loved all the new connections and friendships I was making through this network marketing company. There was just one problem, I was still working at my job and I didn't want to do that anymore. My network marketing side gig was fulfilling me in ways my job wasn't. I was helping people, leading, inspiring, I was having fun and making new friends.

The thought of leaving my job consumed me. One side was me saying; "Life is short girl, do what makes you happy", the other was saying "Girl, you got a kid in college, don't be crazy". Then I started to consider; I love and believe in the products, and I'm extremely impressed with the compensation plan and what I was generating with only working it part-time. My friend Kimberly was doing this full-time and was earning trips, a car, and a six-figure income. If she could do it, why not me?

I started to pray about it. I knew in my heart this is what I was saved for. This is what I'm supposed to be doing. I found my passion and I prayed it would provide. I wasn't even shooting really high. I just saw an opportunity to be my own boss, making the same income or a little more to cover my bills, but most importantly, doing something where I am making a difference in the lives of others.

It was July 2021, seven months after first joining my company that I decided to go for it! I took a leap of faith and went ALL IN! I had played it safe my entire life. In my mind it was the responsible thing to do as I was the sole provider for my kids. Taking this risk was so far out of my comfort zone, but I knew in my heart this is what I was led to do. It was scary. I'd heard a lot of things about this industry. Some good and some bad. I heard no one makes money doing this. I also heard 90% of women making over six-figures are in network marketing. All I knew was I had a great product I believed in, and I believed in me. If I was going to make it to the top of a company, I had the right product to do it with. LET'S DO THIS!

I have a passion for helping women. Women that have lost their spouse, women that have battled cancer, women struggling as a single parent, struggling financially or struggling with their health. I want to inspire her, help her heal, give her hope, and provide an opportunity. This is what I get to do every day! Have you heard the saying "If you love what you do, you'll never work a day in your life"? I found that! There is that something out there for everyone! Sometimes you know what it is but fear stops you from going after it. DON'T LET IT!!

With everything on the line, it was time to get down to business. I was ready to put in the work, be coachable, learn from uplines, sidelines and everyone that had already reached the top. I was willing to do whatever it takes. The number one piece of advice I kept getting was DON'T QUIT! The only way you fail is if you quit! The great thing about network marketing is you could start a business with little to no investment. The bad thing about network marketing is you could start a business with little to no investment. Because you didn't make much of an investment, it's really easy to walk away. Most people quit too soon.

By the time I started working my business full-time I already had a pretty large team, so I set an aggressive goal of the level I wanted to achieve and by when. I didn't have a safety net or back-up plan. What I did have was a kid in college, a ton of debt, and my belief that I can do this! I had to do this! I was not quitting! I laugh as I write this because the thought did cross my mind many times. Doubt comes and starts hanging around and it's up to us to push it away. Stay strong with your belief that yes, YOU CAN DO THIS!

Your environment matters! I had the right product, the right company, it was the right time, and I was on the right team! Who you surround yourself with matters! I truly lucked out to be surrounded by a team of beautiful and positive people that support and encourage each other. With the right people, you grow every day! I was getting out of my comfort zone. I was learning the business from incredible leaders and I was having fun!

I missed my target date by about five months. Honestly, I wasn't disappointed. I was enjoying the journey, my team was growing, and I knew we were doing all the things to make it happen. It was going to happen according to God's perfect plan, and it did! It happened on my birthday month, March! I reached the top of my company! This means so much to me because of all the families it represents that my team and I have impacted! Network Marketing is about building relationships and serving others.

Build your network, build your income. The only way to do that is going for the "No". I remember a moment with a team member I was coaching. She was discouraged with the rejections and was ready to throw in the towel. She had less than 20 team members at the time. With over 200 on my team, I asked her "do you know how many more No's I received to get to 200? Do you know how many No's the top leaders in our company with teams in the thousands had to hear?" My advice on rejection is don't take it personally. Only the strong survive! Don't let rejection slow you down. Keep going!

In my short time in this industry, I've learned a lot. One of those things is that this absolutely works if you work it. You will get out what you put in. If you want to put in one hour a week, I'm confident your income will reflect that. In the same way, if you put in the time like a real business and not a hobby, your income will reflect that as well. I recommend understanding your company's compensation plan, determining how much you want to earn, and then making a game plan on how to achieve it. It's important you understand the compensation plan and all the ways you can earn. If you could earn 5 different ways but you're only earning from one, you're leaving money on the table. Don't do that!

Other than everyone I've helped with our products, I'm most proud of everyone I've helped earn extra life-changing income. On the top of that list are my parents. They are in their 70's, retired and living on a fixed income. They joined me for the business, and earning extra income from the comfort of their home has been a blessing. They've had many unexpected expenses and they are grateful to have the extra funds to cover it. Where else does anyone in their 70's have the opportunity to do that? This has to be my biggest surprise in my business. I never would have imagined I would be working alongside my parents and that they would be rocking this business like two young pros!

My number 1 piece of advice to have success in this business is DON'T QUIT!

The possibilities are endless for you and the teams you lead. I dare you to dream bigger than you ever have. Nothing can stop you when you believe in yourself and you have the right people in your corner supporting you and cheering you on.

God opens doors! You have to take the first step! This too is possible for you!

It's possible to get paid for helping others and serving them with integrity, compassion, and a genuine interest in their needs.

It's possible to make both a living and a difference.

It's possible to inspire, empower, and impact people through the work you do.

This little light of mine, I'm gonna let it shine

Mom, Wife, Mentor, Author, Carrier of Hope and Believer of God's Perfect Timing!

Maria was born and raised in the Bronx to parents that immigrated to the US from the Dominican Republic. At the age of 17 she moved to Miami, Florida where she began working for a company that she would spend more than 30 years with. Maria was married for 17 years and was widowed at 37 years old with three children. Maria is a breast cancer survivor and is passionate about helping all women feel more confidant, believe in themselves and dream bigger than they ever have.
Maria lives in Florida with her partner Willard, their seven-year-old son, Liam, and her youngest daughter Madison. Her oldest daughter, Mariah, is married and lives in Florida with her husband Bob, and her oldest son, Joey, is currently in Germany serving his country with the US Army.

KATHY HENKEN

"The most effective way to get it done is to do it. Continue to push the boundaries of your comfort zone and live the life you dream about."

KATHY HENKEN

In 1996, I attended a product party a friend of mine hosted. I really enjoyed the products and the person that did the demonstration. When she shared with the guests that booking a party would not only help our host earn gifts but give us free products too, I signed up to host one myself. That one party turned into three over the course of the next eighteen months. However, not once during those parties did the representative approach me about doing the business. I didn't know what I didn't know so I didn't think anything of it. I was unaware of the network marketing industry, I assumed it was her job. No one in my family nor anyone I knew was in this profession. Well, if you don't count the lady down the street from us when I was a child. She used to give us miniature white tubes of lipstick to play dress up. Does that ring a bell with anyone?

Almost a decade later, I was helping a friend work her booth of homemade goods at a holiday bazaar. The person in the booth next to us had a lot of people interested in her small line of products. I watched as her calendar filled up rapidly with appointments. Curiosity led me to start asking her questions and we met for coffee several days later. It was with her and the company she was partnered with that I began my network marketing career.

At that time, I had two young daughters and had a corporate job where I worked long hours and traveled several times a month. I knew it put a strain on our family so the possibilities of building a business of my own that allowed me to stay home and replace my income was so exciting! I started working my business part time, alongside my full-time job. A year later, I was able to quit my full-time job. However, five years after enrolling, that company went a different direction, and I didn't have a back-up plan. I loved the freedom and positivity that I had found in marketing and selling products through this business model. Over the next several years I enrolled with three other network marketing companies, but I never felt I found my groove with any of them.

In 2006, my husband transitioned from a corporate job to becoming a small traditional business owner. When the financial crisis of 2008 arrived, it hit us hard. Everything came to a screeching halt. We depleted our retirement funds trying to keep the business afloat. I had gone back into the workforce and was working four part time jobs. From the outside, everything looked the same. No one knew our kids were on free lunch programs. They didn't know I was hiding my car to keep it from being repossessed, or that we were running up credit card debt to pay monthly living expenses. Even though I knew the challenges weren't specific to us and many others were having the same struggle, I wore a shroud of shame. I swear, all my clothing was black in color. . .and everything had hoods.

One afternoon I received a call from someone I hadn't seen in several years. She didn't know what was happening in my life. She called to ask if I had a couple of minutes so she could share something she was excited about with me. It was a newly launched product with results she loved and sold through a network marketing company she loved even more. She wanted to know if she sent me information about the product and the company, would I look at it. I told her I would, but in my head, I was thinking I didn't have the money to purchase what she was offering. When I opened the box and looked through the business information something changed in my head. WHAT IF this is what I'd been praying for? WHAT IF this could change our life situation? WHAT IF this was the box of hope? The WHAT IF changed to WHY NOT?

My desire, willingness to work, and willingness to be coached gave me the confidence to step off and start running right away. It meant making more sacrifices. However, I finally felt like the sacrifices I was making were for my family, not for my employer and their families. I was fortunate to be exposed to personal development in my corporate career by a mentor in that company, not by the corporation itself. I recognized how important personal development is, especially in network marketing, and I started reading and listening to as many books as I was able. I showed up to everything. Every meeting, every training, and every call. It was the best way for me to learn from those who were having the success I wanted. I found mentors along the way. I believe there are very few industries like network marketing where people are so willing to help others succeed.

When I reflect on the last ten years of my network marketing career, I clearly see the highs and lows. I do my best to learn from the lows and have enjoyed riding the wave of the highs. This opportunity changed the trajectory of my life and the life of my family. I have met amazing people and been able to spend more time with those whom I know and love. I have traveled to other countries and explored more of my own country. My daughters have been able to travel with me many times, which has sweetened my experiences even more. It's really hard to pick one moment that I would say is my favorite, but at the top is when I surprised my girls with a trip to Paris. The trip was better than anything we could have imagined. So many wonderful memories!

Something I don't think people truly understand is the value of work merit and time freedom. Many of us have worked jobs where the people with the poorest work ethic and people with the best work ethic are paid the same. It can be deflating. In network marketing, those that have a great work ethic get paid well. Those that have a poor work ethic, or who don't work at all, get paid poorly or don't get paid. We are required to put in the time to make an income like we may have never made before, but it is so worth it!

Time freedom is something many people have never experienced. Most jobs require you to trade your time for money. Network marketing allows you to work in and around your life. When we have vacations to plan, I don't have to worry about asking for the time off. Most of the time I can do business while on vacation. It is such a blessing to have the time freedom I have because of my business. It has allowed me to take my nephew to chemo treatments for a year, be with him and comfort him and his family as he passed. His wife would have lost her job if she took that much time away. I'm so grateful to have been able to support my daughter and her husband when she delivered our miracle grandson, Baylor, three months early. As a micro-preemie, he spent eighty-five days in the NICU, with his parents by his side for fourteen hours a day. They didn't have to stress about issues at home because my business allowed me the time freedom to help. I am also able to take care of my two-year-old grandson, Baker, two days a week because I can devote time to my business with him in my care. These have been some of the biggies, but smaller things happen daily that don't require me to have to make a choice between my business and my family. I can work my business in the cracks and crevices of my day.

I have learned that no one gets to the top by themselves. You must help others get what they want and need to have your dreams fulfilled. My biggest surprise is always how much people respect you when you do that. The more you recognize and value others, the more you are respected and valued.

Have you read the book *The Slight Edge* by Jeff Olson? This philosophy is no joke. Success is built over time with small disciplines executed on a consistent basis with a good attitude. It's not magic. Anyone can do it, but most won't. Creating positive habits, especially work habits, will help you build an income you never thought possible. This business model is so simple, but it is not always easy. I have worked hard to develop a business that is woven in and around my life. It has generated residual income that keeps the money monkey off my back. It has allowed me so many incredible choices to do what makes me happy while serving others.

The past two years, living through a pandemic, have taught me many things. Human connection is like oxygen. We don't thrive long without it. The world learned to adapt to stay connected, and this business model survived with flying colors, especially with the use of tech support and social media. It brought another platform for us to connect and help others that was under-utilized. As the world begins to open back up, I see opportunities to become better everywhere.

There are many activities that, when done together, will create momentum in your business. These are the ones I consider to be at the top.

- ***Be wildly curious about others.*** Learn to ask questions. People will tell you a lot about themselves when they know you care about getting to know them. It's much easier to be a solution provider when you understand someone's needs.

- ***Ask, without judgment,*** if they will accept your offer to share what you have with them. Think of it like this. . . A waiter in a restaurant asks everyone, every time they are seated, if they would like a beverage. They don't decide if the customer should or shouldn't have a beverage. And when the customer says no, they don't take it personally. They know the person's decision has nothing to do with them. They move to the next table. If the same person returns the next day, they ask again. No one thinks it's weird. But if the waiter tried to convince the customer to pick a beverage or didn't ask at all, that may result in an awkward situation. So just keep asking. So many successful people in this profession were asked multiple times, over a long period of time, by the same person before they said yes to enrolling. Timing is everything. When someone says no to my offer, I always ask "Does no mean no, not right now, or does it mean no, I'd rather chew glass." Have a sense of humor and a good attitude. If they say "No means not right now", ask for their permission to follow up with them later.

- ***Follow up! Follow up! Follow up!*** It's said the fortune is in the follow up. It's an activity that creates success in most things. Our book of business depends on us sharing with people and following up with them.

- ***Prepare to fail.*** No one is exempt from failure, particularly in this industry. Learn from your failures and take note of what you don't want to repeat. Imagine you are a baby learning to walk. You will fall down a lot in the beginning, but you continue to get better with each fall. Don't give up!

- ***Be consistent with your daily business habits***. It is one of the simplest things to do, but one of the easiest things not to do. Use a planner to track your activities. It will show you where you are doing well and where you need to improve.

I am so happy I said "yes" to the person that shared with me and I'll be forever grateful to her. The success I've had with the company I joined has changed my life, my family's lives and the thousands of customers and business partners in my organization. I have met incredible people, traveled to amazing places and have time freedom that allows me to spend my days doing what fulfills me. I am surrounded with positive people that are focused on helping others. All because someone asked me to look at what they had to offer.

If I could go back in time when I first started my business, the thing I would do differently is ask MORE people FASTER! I was fearful in the beginning that people would judge me, so I didn't ask as many people as I should have. Develop the attitude of not wanting someone to be disappointed in you because you didn't think to share with them. Share, not convince, and let them decide. Don't make the decision for them. Regardless of the outcome, they will thank you for offering.

Follow a business model that creates duplication and empowers others, and you will be able to build daily confidence in yourself and your business.

Kathy grew up in Seattle, Washington. The oldest of seven children, she attributes many of her strengths to her birth order. She considers one of her strengths to be her great interpersonal skills, empowering her to help others look, feel and live better. She loves to travel, watch movies, play games, cook and spend time with friends and family, especially two little grandsons that call her Mimi. She and her husband recently moved to Boise, Idaho and are enjoying the high desert life.

"What if

this is what you've been

praying for?"

JODY MALEY

"You cannot lead your tribe from the back."

JODY MALEY

I was actually raised in an entrepreneurial family. Growing up, my dad was a teacher/coach in our local high school as well as my coach for gymnastics. My mom was, for the most part, a stay-at-home mom, but would always have a part-time job and contributed when she could.

As I was growing up my parents always had some kind of second income from a network marketing business. Throughout our youth, my two older brothers and I were dragged to many conventions and workshops all over Canada and the United States. So, I had a blend of highly competitive and entrepreneurial skills that took me into my teens and my early twenties.

I started with my first networking company in my early twenties while my two older children were quite young (I'm a mom of six with a blended family… two his, two mine and two together). At that time in my life, I didn't dream of wealth and how to grow my business, I literally joined because I needed adult conversation and to get out of the house.

The first business I joined was in direct sales and hosting home parties. Since I was about 8 hours away from my upline I relied on the company's corporate manual and learned from there how to do home parties. I think the benefit of this is that I learned how to have my own style, to keep my presentations short and to really connect one on one with my hostesses and customers.

My sales took off and I was continually having around $1,000 parties with about 3-4 new hostesses from each show. Then I 'accidentally' entered leadership. I didn't really want to recruit people as I had seen my parents have a focus on just 'getting people to sign up' and then introduce the product. I wanted my business to be more focused on show sales, customer retention and having fun!

So, when a guest came up to me and said "I've been watching you and I want to join your team" I was stunned. In a few short months I added a few new people to my team and decided to learn more about how to be a great leader. Lucky for me I had a great upline leader from whom I could truly learn. I learned how to be a business leader and to teach business skills quickly to ladies who were joining my team.

I knew from watching my parents over the years how burn out and constantly putting money into their various businesses cost them thousands and thousands. I wanted more for myself and my team. I developed a model that if I wasn't profitable and having fun ... for me and my team ... I would stop! After all, the whole point of having a business was to be there for my kids and not miss the important parts of their lives.

A funny story that still has me giggling to this day was the first ever convention I attended as an adult. I remember being in awe that the speakers were other moms just like myself. Average, ordinary women who were making a big impact through this company. You see, up until then the Conventions I attended had big speakers like Tony Robbins, Jay Van Andel, Zig Ziglar and Robert Kiyosaki to name just a few.

I remember when one of the speakers came on stage and she said, "Who here ever dreamed that one day they'd grow up to be an entrepreneur?" Well, I jumped out of my seat, raised my hand and gave a big whoop and a "hell yeah"... only to be the only one in that group of about 500 ladies who did. Everyone laughed and I got dubbed for the rest of the Convention as the "hell yeah" girl from BC.

It was then that it dawned on me how truly differently I was raised and brought up. I mean I grew up drawing business circles to my Barbies on mini chalk boards when I was like eight or nine years old. Having sales conversations with adults in my teens while negotiating babysitting co-ops and organizing my friends to help was second nature. I even remember firing a piano teacher I had when I was sixteen, insisting to my parents that if she didn't believe in me why should we be paying her?

It was sitting there in that audience that I put forth an intention that next year, at this time I would be on stage, I would be sharing how I became the number one salesperson in the country and sharing that.

Guess what? Powerful intentions combined with intentional actions lead to powerful outcomes. I immediately found my upline that I admired and said to her "Is it possible for me to be on that stage next year? And can you show me how?" I remember her smiling and looking at me directly in the eye and saying these words I will never forget ... "Yup, but I'm warning you right now it won't be easy and you have to commit to doing 100% exactly what I say no questions asked. Do you agree?" We shook hands and in the next six months I did exactly what she told me to do.

The next year I was indeed on that stage. I was a new leader and continued to break sales records and was asked to speak about how to motivate new recruits. I remember standing there before a Convention crowd of nearly 800 women and asking if they remembered from the year before this question "Who ever dreamed of one day being an entrepreneur?" and if they remembered the crazy girl who jumped up and said "hell yeah" while everyone else laughed?

Many people remembered and still laughed about that and I just stood proudly and said "yup, that was me a year ago ... and yes, I always dreamed of being a successful entrepreneur and leader and today I'm going to teach you some of the skills I have learned so that you too can achieve the greatness you deserve!" No one laughed at me that weekend! Haha!

You see, being an entrepreneur does require a bit of a different mindset. Sometimes you grow up with it, but many people … I'd say about 90 per cent of the population has to be introduced to it. For myself as a young twenty something it was that yearning deep inside that kept nagging at me and questioning "Is this really all my life is going to be? How can I truly help someone else? What could I give to someone else to help change their lives?"

I stayed with that company for several more years learning how to continue to grow my team and my leadership skills … while facing several life challenges. Like a divorce, custody battle, new spouse, step kids and even our house burning to the ground! Here's the funny thing with life challenges, and I firmly believe this, you have two choices when going through these challenges:

1. Complain to everyone you know and keep the drama going or
2. Learn from the challenge and grow so that you are in the rare position to help someone else going through the same challenge.

I have ALWAYS chosen choice number 2.

It was at the end of working with this amazing company that I faced a real-life challenge and to this day I still sit in awe of how it has changed and motivated me to be the real leader and inspiration I want to be in the world.

I had taken some training on being a personality coach and was pregnant with kiddo number 6 when my doctor put me on complete bed rest for several weeks before my son was born and then several weeks after. Now this was over 18 years ago, and we didn't have all the cool stuff we have now to keep in contact with customers and team members. It was literally me and my phone and my stack of rolodex cards.

But after working so hard for nine years to build my business, not just once but three times, I absolutely refused to give up this extra income. So, every day I made several calls from my bed. To past customers, to past hostesses and to ladies in my downline I hadn't even met yet in person.

I didn't know at the time that the company was running a huge yearly promotion and that those leaders who increased their business by over 20% at the end of the year would win this huge award. I just did what I had to do, to keep my baby healthy, safe, and alive, and to keep my business afloat.

It was a rough year; I faced a lot of negativity from my upline and downline that I wasn't keeping up to par. That I wasn't hosting trainings like I should, that I wasn't going to the annual convention. I just felt that I wasn't up to snuff on everything! But every month I'd talk to the trainer the company assigned to me. She'd tell me not to worry, she knew I was doing the best that I could do and that taking care of my health and the health of my new baby was truly the best I could do and to keep up the good work.

I would bring new consultants with me to host shows when my doctor finally said I could get up and around, and I continued my daily calls to keep my team and business afloat. My beautiful baby boy was born at the end of April with another few months of bedrest as I was severely anemic.

Fall came and I continued on the same path, using my new skills as a personality coach to help, train and motivate my team.

At the end of the year, I was told by my trainer that I had qualified for the trip incentive by increasing my business by 20%. Here's the irony, I didn't want to go. I felt that because of the negative feedback I had from other leaders and my team that I didn't deserve this trip.

My spouse convinced me to go, after all it was completely paid for. He said he had everything at home taken care of, our youngest was now over 8 months old, and that he wanted me to take this week-long break.

I flew from beautiful BC all the way to Toronto and thought I would take this opportunity to learn from all these amazing leaders in the company. There were over 140 other leaders who had increased their business by over 20% in the past year and I thought how great and awesome it would be for me to learn even more.

I made it my sole purpose to find out who the top 5 were in this group of ladies so that I could sit by them for breakfast, lunch and dinner so I could even get some more tips and ideas. I remember carrying around my little black notebook so I could record their names and where they were from.

On the big event and award night I remember the President of the company had the top 5 ladies from across Canada come up to receive their awards and she said how much they had increased their personal and team sales in the last year. Let me tell you, I was fervently writing down their names so I wouldn't miss time with any of them. It was amazing! Some had increased their business by 30 and 40% and the second top lady had increased hers by over 60%.

I was amazed that I was even sitting in the same room as these superstars. Then she said the top person and leader in Canada who had increased her business by a whopping 148% is … and I was glued to my black notebook thinking "holy crap who is this superstar?" and then she called my name.

Shock and disbelief went through my system. I remember looking around the room like there must be someone else with the name of Jody haha! I remember going up to receive this award and all the feelings overwhelming me … I just didn't deserve this.

When the President of the company shook my hand, she whispered in my ear… "I know exactly what your last year looked like and the struggles you faced to get here … and I'm telling you that you did not WIN this trip you EARNED it, and you DESERVE it".

I seriously cannot even write this without tears in my eyes right now! This was one of those moments in my life that made such a huge impact for myself and for the hundreds of women who I have helped since then.

Over the next few days of training, I really reflected on 'who I wanted to be and who I wanted to serve'. The biggest thing that stood out to me then and still stands true in my heart is this:

How many other women have stood to receive something truly great and magnificent in their lives and felt that they just didn't deserve it?

How many other amazing leaders, entrepreneurs, wives and moms have done extraordinary things in their lives and have felt undeserving of the accolades?

I know that I sure did! And I decided to take ownership that day of my greatness! That even though I stepped out in a different way to leadership and my own personal sales, that I had accomplished more in that year then I had ever done before and that I truly EARNED it.

It may have felt messy to me, it may have been different than how any other leader did it, but the fact is I did accomplish it. And, I was determined that no other woman on the face of this planet should ever feel that they are undeserving of the best in their lives, their family or their health!

Sometimes we have to do something so vastly different to realize the greatness we have within us!

Sometimes we have to look at ourselves and say "hey, this wasn't the outcome I expected, this wasn't the clean and easy way to do something, but look at what I accomplished! Against the odds, against the negativity, against my own self doubt".

Has my life been perfect since? Of course not!

I've been lucky enough to be in a few different companies since then! I've made some great money, I've built strong teams, and I've failed at a few too.

I've taken my love of sales and leadership into some brick-and-mortar companies as well because I wanted to see if what I teach and do could work there too! Guess what? It does! In one furniture company I sold over 2 million dollars worth of product in 18 months!

When things looked crappy, or I felt I didn't deserve my accomplishments I always bring it back to what I did in that year of increasing my business by 148%? What stood out? What is it that I can continue to train and lead on?

Simple! People matter! Having a daily connection with 5-6 people and reaching out to them is what mattered! Letting a client, customer or team member know that I am there for them is what continues to matter to this day!

In this day and age where we think it's all about systems, where we think it's about having thousands of connections is how we make the big bucks.

I'm here to say that isn't what matters at all! Don't get me wrong, systems help support us and having a continual list of people to talk to can bring you more. But there is nothing more satisfying and more 'on purpose' with your vision and your integrity than by having an authentic conversation where you know you truly helped and served and in some small way just made someone's day a little bit brighter!

People will often join a business because they love the product or service, but they will stay with a company when they are making an income. And trust me my friend, you may think that what you are doing may seem small or insignificant, but it isn't! You are changing lives, you are making a legacy for yourself, your family and more importantly for the team you want to build!

You got this, because amazing leaders like myself have got you!

If I could impart one piece of advice that I would give myself years ago it would be this:

Align yourself with a great coach, leader or trainer who can bring out the most in YOU! I am always investing in myself in some way. For a few years it was having a personal development coach and immersing in a 'million dollar a year' women's club.

If ever I felt 'comfortable' I knew it was time to hire someone who could kick me up a notch. When I struggle with health, I hire a health coach. If I struggled with marketing, I'd hire a marketing coach.

Don't try to wear all the hats required in a business. Find out where you are the greatest and possess the most skills, then hire where you are the weakest to fill in the gaps!

Here's my Quote when asked what I thought being a Great Leader meant:

"You're willing to take the steps, you're willing to better yourself, you're willing to do the training first before you lead others toward what your vision, your ideas, and what your products are!"

What really sets a GREAT leader apart from the others is their willingness to show their team how to do something by leading the way, doing the things, setting the examples and bettering themselves.

You simply cannot lead your tribe from the back!

What really sets a GREAT leader apart from the others is their willingness to show their team how to do something by leading the way, doing the things, setting the examples and bettering themselves.

JERI TAYLOR-SWADE

"Just Keep on Keeping on!"

"If it is going to be, it is up to me!"

JERI TAYLOR-SWADE

Creating a legacy by having a "Keep On Keeping On" mindset

"One of the most challenging aspects of a home-based business is to keep going! "Keep on Keeping on!" Keep yourself on track, keep moving forward and keep motivated for years. If you want a sustainable business that you can build a legacy on, there are definite steps to achieve what you want. It's one thing to stay "UP" and motivated when you first start your business. The test comes when disappointments and obstacles come your way. Those are the times that the true GRIT of who you are and what you want comes into play. You have a choice to make: You must decide if you are committed! It's up to you. YOU are the one that will make or break your business. Through being persistent and consistent, and taking action to do the "work", you will succeed. Bottom line...Successful people do what Unsuccessful people won't do and Successful people don't quit. They find a way." ~Jeri Taylor-Swade

Since you are reading this book, I am guessing you are new to Direct Sales and trying to glean as much information and knowledge as possible...OR you have been in the Direct Sales/MLM/Network Marketing industry for a long time and you are looking for motivation and encouragement. Either way, I think I can help you! HI! My name is Jeri Taylor-Swade and I have been in this amazing career of Direct Sales for 24 years now. Can you believe I have stayed with the same company all that time? Yes, I am proud of both of those facts, however behind them (24 years and same company) is a tremendous amount of hours, investment, seeking, learning, doubting, and persisting. Some say it takes 10,000 hours to master a skill, or to be "great" at something. In my opinion, as far as Network Marketing is concerned, it takes 6-10 years to fully master this industry. It all depends on how much time, effort, learning and mistakes you make along the way. When you first start out, you are so dang excited, motivated and ready to conquer the world and then REALITY sets in! You actually have to do the WORK! That "work" is determined by the company you are with, the products you represent, and what your goals of achievement are. In order for your company to be legitimate, it must be Product-centric, which means you are representing products to consumers. The basic WORK of doing that is where so many fail after some time. Usually you start sharing, talking, demonstrating and promoting those products, as well as talking about the opportunity to your family and friends first. As you do this, some are responsive, they listen, and because of your enthusiasm and belief in your representation of the products and company, they purchase from you and some may also decide to join your team! YOU ARE SO EXCITED! Wow, I did it! I am on my way!" you say! THEN the reality of what every person who has ever done this business marketing strategy sets in. You don't know who else to talk to, and the "Team" that you have created, doesn't either. I am not here to talk about the steps to take next, as there are so many books, podcasts, seminars etc. that teach that.

What I am here to speak about is something that I have learned from going through it, learning the next steps to take, and HOW to keep going! In my office, on the wall right in front of me as I write this, in BIG letters is written "Keep ON Keeping ON". This is my motto, my team's motto and the motto I live by outside of business. Truly, if you grasp this, you WILL succeed! Keep ON Keeping ON is an Idiom, a phrase, a "saying" that you have heard, but have you really stopped to think about what it actually means? It means Don't Quit! There have been times over the years I have had to say this to myself "Quitters Quit, am I a Quitter?" and I've had to answer that question! NO, I AM NOT A QUITTER!. Once I have answered that question, then the next step I take is to figure out what I had to do to NOT Quit! I have learned that it always requires action on my part. The tough part is figuring out what action that is and then doing it. Usually for me, it goes back to the basics of business.

I feel so strongly about Keep On Keeping On! Within those four words lies the secret of success! Keeping On is the act of doing what you have been doing with continuousness. It is being Persistent and Consistent. It is continuing or repeating behavior that moves you forward. The challenge is to ALWAYS find the inner strength, motivation and resolve to do it. Ask any successful athlete, actor or entrepreneur, and you will find that the theme throughout his/her success is the determination to not give up. It takes GRIT. It takes being tenacious. It takes "doggedness", which means going after what you want like a "Dog on a Bone".

Many, many songs, poems, and stories have been written about Keeping ON. Why? Because they all realize that you must have that Never Give Up mindset. You keep fighting even when you feel that losing is inevitable. You keep fighting. You keep going. You keep trying. You keep moving. You Keep On Keeping ON! Persistence is so key to becoming excellent at something. It is simply the quality of always continuing to move forward EVEN when you don't feel like it. It means you continue regardless of setbacks. The difference between a long-term winner in this business is that you do what you don't want to do, but know you MUST do it! I can't tell you how many times over the years that I literally have raised my hands in the air and said out loud "I won't give up! If it is going to be, it is up to me!" I realized when it came down to it, that my success was about ME and what I do, not about relying on others. I realized long ago that it was my attitude that makes the difference.

When you are in Network Marketing, you build a team. Those team members come and go. It is a good leader that can keep a team together, as there is this thing called Attrition, which means team members leave the business. They leave for all sorts of reasons, however, in my experience, they leave because they are "stuck"; they don't want to do the "work" anymore, or in reality, life happens, and they give up or just plain don't want to do it anymore. In that case (through my experience), they didn't have enough belief in themselves, they didn't understand their "why" in a deeper way that would sustain the business. They didn't have enough belief in the products, the company they are with, or the Business Model of MLM. Sometimes they leave because they have been convinced that the "Grass is Greener on the other side". This is a sad one, because MOST of the time, in my experience, they jump from one company to another, thinking it will be more profitable, or that they will have a leader that will be better etc., but what they find, is that it comes down to the same thing...you have to work! You have to put time and effort into building a sustainable business.

Passion and the love of what you are doing, the love of the products you represent and the love of the company you are associated with is HUGE! YOU MUST be PASSIONATE! It gives you the basis to fall back on when you feel like you are faltering. It is your foundation. That foundation is there when you get discouraged. Everyone gets down. Everyone goes through ups and downs! It is normal! The key is to keep going when you are down and know the steps to get back up and moving again! I have had to do this so many times in the years of being in Direct Sales! Trust me, it isn't easy! You've heard the term, "Pull yourself up by your bootstraps"? That term is another Idiom that basically means that you improve your situation by hard work and self-determination. You need to be willing to get up every day and do what it takes.

Building a Legacy through having a "Keep On Keeping On" mindset means that you kept persevering, you kept persisting! It means that even when Life happens and you may have to step back, or take a break, you ALWAYS get up, get out and start moving again! When you do this, the magic happens! You start making money, friends, gaining confidence, achieving goals and building a sustainable business. In my company, I am proud to have achieved many awards, traveled the world, made money, made lasting lifetime relationships and friends with not only my team, others in the company, but also my customers. I built a sustainable business, but honestly none of that matters more than the affect I have had on my family! When I started in this business of Network Marketing/Direct Sales, my kids were still in school! Both of them worked for me in some capacity over the years. They saw me achieve and be rewarded greatly for my hard work. They experienced my emotional times when I thought I just wanted to give up. They saw me pull myself up and put myself "out there" again. They learned great lessons of persistence and perseverance, and today, as I see my adult children with families of their own, they have great attitudes, they are successful, they have confidence and they know if they want something in life, they have to work for it. Building a Legacy is about life and living. It's about learning from the past, living in the present and building for the future.

Every person leaves a legacy, whether they know it or not. You can leave a positive, powerful one, or leave a sad one. Some think leaving a legacy is about leaving money or personal belongings to the next generation. It is so much more than that! To me it's about when I'm long gone, what am I remembered for? Have I made a lasting impact on those who have come in contact with me throughout my life? In business, you will be known for what you have accomplished, but also if you had integrity, how you treated people. If you were fair. If you always did the right thing, and if you didn't, did you say you were sorry? You will be known for how generous you were with your time and your finances. You will be remembered for the tangible awards and accolades you achieved etc. In your life, with your family and those around you outside of business, basically you will be remembered for all of the above, however, you will be remembered and held up in history for generations to come by how much you loved, how much you cared, what practical life-lessons you taught, what "sayings" you had that will be repeated even when you are gone. You will be remembered for the faith you had, how much you served others, your smile, joy and zest for life and your kindness. Your legacy is your ability to make others feel good and create positive ripples that last a long time. If you are a man or woman of Faith, you will be remembered by how you lived that out in your life. You will be remembered by how devoted you were to your God, and others.

Most think of leaving a Legacy in a tangible, monetary-valued way. As that is absolutely true, there is more to leaving a Legacy. The "intangible gifts" that you leave behind for your family, friends or community are priceless. As I write this, I am 67 years young, and I think about it and make decisions on the "Legacy" principles every day. When looking at my life through the Legacy lens, it makes a difference in the choices I make. My husband and I love life; we have fun. We travel. We lack nothing; however, we don't have the "It's our money, it's our resources, it's our pleasures" attitude. We are always conscious of the fact that our grown children and grandchildren watch us. We give back and we pay forward those things monetarily and otherwise to them and others. Our kids and grandkids know we love them; they can count on us and we are truly interested in them. My husband and I have been blessed through our careers, mine in Direct Sales and his in the IT industry. We have been able to buy houses, rentals, our own home, drive nice cars, have a nest egg for retirement, go on amazing vacations around the world (and take our grandkids too!), and still give back to our family, our church and our community. Being a blessing to others is a Legacy to which we aspire.

You could definitely say in my career as a Direct Seller I have earned a lot, achieved a lot, and I'm leaving a Legacy. I'm not saying this to brag, but to encourage and motivate you because those achievements you've worked for and earned matter!

I have achieved many "firsts" in my company. I have been an innovator, a leader and motivator to those on my team, to others in the company, to other Direct Sellers outside of my company and to my customers as well. The CEO of my company actually has stated many times "There goes Jeri again with another 1st!" I have achieved the highest rank (at the time) in the company and was the only one to maintain that title for 14 of the 24 years I have been a Direct Seller. My motto is known throughout the world in my company "Just Keep on Keeping On!" I am a record-breaker and have been known as a "Distributor Advocate" who has stood up to Corporate in defense or championed for "The Field". Integrity is a big part of this, and it is one facet of Legacy that is huge! I could go on and on about me, but in all honesty, as I think back and into the future of my life, my priority is to be proud of what I've done, always aware of the fact I could have done more or been better, but very happy that along the way I have been an inspiration and blessing to others. When leaving a Legacy, looking back to see what kind of an impact you have made in all aspects of life and being happy about it is monumental. My advice: Take an assessment of your life so far. Look at your family, your career, your community and your internal, spiritual person. Do you like what you see? If you died tomorrow, what would you have left behind, both tangible and intangible, that would have blessed others? What would those that know you say about you? If you don't like what you see in the assessment of yourself, YOU CAN DO SOMETHING ABOUT IT! Start today to make the changes. Start today. Purposefully give your time and wisdom to others. Be on purpose with your career. Work intentionally every day! NEVER give up no matter what. It is time to decide. Right now, you must decide that no matter what, you will keep going! You will "Keep on Keeping On!" You must decide what kind of a legacy you want to create. In order to create a powerful legacy, you need to have urgency about it. No one knows how much time they have left. Decide what matters most and GO FOR IT! Step it up in your business and in your life!

Decide what action you need to take to achieve the things in life you say you want. Make a list and if you need help, reach out to someone who wants more for you too. The key is to be willing to make changes if necessary. Be flexible and teachable. Sometimes it takes a re-evaluation of yourself. Sometimes you need to shift your thinking. Take action steps that will move you forward. Go to a seminar or training that will give you knowledge and building blocks. Most of all, DO THE WORK! It is so worth it.

"I believe my key to success is having GRIT...consistency, persistence, perseverance, and the ability to establish and maintain a phenomenal team." ~ Jeri Taylor-Swade

With no knowledge or understanding of the direct sales/network marketing world, Jeri started out as a "part time" distributor 24 years ago in 1999. Now, Jeri is a Master of Beauty & Business, Direct Sales/Party Plan Expert, Founding Pioneer in her company and has earned the title given to her by newer Distributors as the "Original OG". She drives a Company Car, too.

Jeri has earned so many of the incentive trips she has lost count but suffice to say she has traveled the world because of the Direct Selling Company that she represents. Jeri is a Certified International Trainer, Motivator & Elite Makeup Artist.

Jeri was recognized as an inspiring leader and was given the Annual TOP Motivator award in 2004. Just this year, she was recognized worldwide in her company as a "Record Breaker" for the 2nd time. Jeri is an author, podcaster, certified Toastmaster, and pioneered the very 1st DSWA (Direct Selling Women's Alliance) chapter in the USA and held the office of president in Las Vegas for 7 years.

Jeri has built a Legacy in her company and is part of the history forever, and now she focuses on building a Legacy for her family.

I believe my key to success is having GRIT…consistency, persistence, perseverance, and the ability to establish and maintain a phenomenal team.

DARLENE NEUFELD

"Never let a ten-cent problem destroy a million-dollar attitude."

DARLENE NEUFELD

"That is the last thing I would do". I was right.

I was first approached about direct sales after my first child was born. I was on maternity leave and looking forward to when I would go back to my government job. I shot down the suggestion with an emphatic "That's the last thing I would do!" Luckily for me, the person I was talking to had an incredible amount of persistence.

She pointed out that when you add up the cost of childcare, transportation and parking, lunches, clothes for work, and lack of sleep, I probably wouldn't make enough money to make up for missing those important firsts with my child. Although I said no several times, she refused to accept that answer. Reluctantly, I decided to give it a try. I knew I would fail miserably, but would have proven to my husband that I was happiest when I worked outside of the home.

I LOVED BEING IN DIRECT SALES! I was there for all our son's important firsts and even had a second child to enjoy. Because it was "party plan" direct sales company, I was home during the day, loving the time with him. I could enjoy a nutritious family supper, then put him in his dad's hands while I went to do a party. I had important interaction with people, while building critical interpersonal skills. I had control over my time and the freedom to say, "today is time for me". The training from the company was fantastic. As I helped team members build on their talents, I earned trips, merchandise, and an income that soon over-shadowed my husband's. I was earning more money than I would have if I had gone back to my government job! As a result of my success, we even had an opportunity to re-locate to run one of the company's top distribution centers in Canada! All in all, it was a great investment in my personal growth.

When you have experience in sales, so many opportunities open up to you! Back in Winnipeg, someone spoke to me about a fledgling bottled-water franchise. This was when buying water for drinking and cooking, instead of relying on the public water system, was just starting to catch on. A franchise is just another form of direct sales. Recognizing that it was a golden opportunity to enter at the ground floor of a new consumer trend, I jumped in. It represented a HUGE financial commitment. Because my husband wasn't sold on the idea, I had to finance it on my own. The debt burden was overwhelming, but thankfully I had the financial management, and interpersonal skills to meet the challenge. To succeed in sales, you want to learn time management, goal setting, and adopt the attitude that failure is not an option! I would need that determination because I fell and broke my foot less than 3 months after opening my store. All the skills I had developed with the party plan company now came into play.

Remember, this was at a time when buying water wasn't a routine event for city dwellers. In the beginning, I had NO customers, but lots of bills. So, I had to educate people on WHY they should spend their hard-earned money on water when there was a kitchen faucet in every home. During the times when people weren't coming in, I would grab a phone book (we had them back then), pick a letter of the alphabet, and start looking for names that were in my area. I would phone people and offer to bring them a FREE bottle of our pure, distilled water. There were lots of "no's" (typical for direct sales) but my experience told me to shake them off because a "yes" wasn't far away. When I would deliver to the people who said yes, I would ask to come in and explain why this bottle of water was such a special gift. My experience in direct sales gave me the confidence to ask for that time and sell the benefits of my product. Seven years after opening up that franchise outlet, I was given the award of "Entrepreneur of the Year-Franchisee Category" by Women Business Owners of Manitoba. I had managed to pay off all my start-up costs and even upgrade equipment to handle my growing sales. Was it hard work? Of course! But the rewards were worth it.

Unfortunately, the franchise was bought out. The new master franchisor did not have the integrity that the original franchisor had. I sold my store on the promise that he had a job at head office waiting for me. Three days after the new owners took possession of my store, he reneged on that offer. That was an important learning experience for me. It taught me that when it comes to company management, you really have to look at the character of the person at the top. Does he/she really have the interests of the "little guy" at heart? I would see many more examples of shallow, self-serving company owners in the years ahead.

Over the years, the Direct Sales industry has changed. More and more, companies have moved to a Network Marketing or MLM (Multi Level Marketing) business model. Even the party plan company I cut my "selling teeth" on has moved to that business model. I think it is because it is reflective of the now defunct store chains like Sears. People are quick to call MLM a pyramid scheme. NOT TRUE. But, just like the Sears store, you have a Head Office (owners of the main business), then outlets (teams of sales people). Every, outlet has a Store Manager (if you aren't one of the original recruiters for the business, it's your "up, up line"). Every store has departments with a Department Head (in MLM, these are the recruits of the "up, up line"). Each Department Head has people working under him/her. These are the newest recruits, who are out with the people, promoting the products. Just as a new hire in a department store can work hard and rise among the ranks to a Department Head or Store Manager, someone new in a MLM can rise up the ranks. It all depends on your drive and hard work.

These days, you can buy just about anything online through an MLM company. There's science-based skincare, supplements, kitchen products and culinary supplies. You may ask yourself, why do people make the decision to sell their inventions, scientific discoveries, etc. via direct sales? The answer is simple. People will buy from people they know and trust. If it is a high-end product or especially a science-based product, people need to be educated as to why they should spend more when a cheaper model is available from another company. The cost to sell or educate via a television commercial is astronomical. So, companies have decided they would rather reward individuals for their dedication in promoting their product than help an advertising agency get rich. Besides, there's no guarantee that the right people will see a TV ad. Whereas, when someone talks to a potential customer, that one-on-one connection is there. Word of mouth sells.

So how do you decide on which MLM to join? There are many factors to consider:

1. **What is the product?** Is it something where there are dozens of other companies selling the same kind of product? That's a lot of competition to handle! What sets that product apart from all its competitors? How will you inspire consumers to make the switch? You could be fighting an uphill battle.

2. **Is this something that will be around for a while?** Is it unique? Is it a new consumer trend? When I bought my distilled water franchise, I read everything I could get my hands on about the subject of distilled water and the state of public water supplies. I had to feel certain that the need for the product was lasting.

3. **What is the management team or company culture like?** For me this is a big consideration. Over the years I have learned that compensation plans and culture are different from company to company. Best to find the one that is most suited to you.

4. **Can you get excited about the product(s)?** It's your passion for the product and the company that will sell it. It's your passion that will encourage you to risk another 'no' to call another prospect. It's your passion that will inspire you to expand well beyond your comfort zone walls and explore new ways to make your business grow.

I have been in the direct sales industry for decades, learning and preparing for the future. Five years ago, all that experience paid off. I found a company and product line that checked all the boxes. I am passionate about the company, the technology, and the products. It will definitely be the last company I promote.

Can you see? I love helping people. I love educating people about something they probably have never heard of before but something that will become as commonplace as a cell phone. I love spending extra time with customers to improve their quality of life. It is very much like when I was educating consumers as to why they would want to pay for bottled water. The feedback I get from my customers makes it all worthwhile. They are so pleased they are telling their friends and helping my business grow.

Direct sales, whether you call it MLM, Network Marketing, franchising or retail selling is all about connecting with people in a meaningful way. Some of it is done all online, but it can never take the place of word-of-mouth. If you want to get paid ***what YOU are worth,*** jump in and join us.

Darlene Neufeld is a wife, mother and grandmother. She has been an entrepreneur for over 40 years. "Lucky for me, someone persisted in helping me realize that entrepreneurism is a respected career choice that gives you the best job security ever. YOU are the only person that can fire you. Downsizing and budget constraints cannot take your job from you. You can shape it to fit your family and lifestyle".

With a ready smile, she approaches life with energy and a great sense of humor. "I believe you can have FUN while working hard". She embraces the people she meets and tells them she will match their efforts 100% in helping them build a successful business.

CHANDRA DUBAY

"When you wrap your head around your life, then you will make your life!"

CHANDRA DUBAY

Throw away that DAMN mirror

I don't care how googly-eyed, pimply-faced, stringy-haired, fat, skinny, or ugly you think you are, TRUST me you are NOT! I don't care what your parents, siblings, aunts, uncles, or friends did or did not do or say to you, because trust me YOU are in control of how that affects YOU.

I'm here to talk about the network marketing profession, how I came to be involved in it, and how I am succeeding and helping others do the same. BUT- I have to tell you, YOU are in control of the outcome, always.

So, let's begin at the beginning.

The baby of five girls, with the next oldest being ten years my senior, I'm just a Prairies farm girl who grew up on a farm in northern Saskatchewan in Canada. I rode a bus to and from school for twenty minutes, which some days were sheer hell.

I was shy, meek and mild. Always wanting to be the "teacher pleaser" and was teased about it over and over and over again. While riding the bus every day, I dreaded if one certain girl would sit by me. She would pinch my hand until I had a huge bruise on it, every day! I was too embarrassed to speak up even when my parents asked who was doing this to me. You see, back then, I didn't know I had a right or a voice.

STAY WITH ME – we'll come back to that *DAMN mirror*!

However, in the circle of my parent's friends, I was loved immensely and spoiled, being the baby of the family. I started selling in the network marketing industry even back then; catalogues sales of greeting cards, paper and trinkets. Then, in junior high, on to higher end items but still catalogue sales. In high school, I got into the makeup industry, still catalogue sales ....

Moving to a small town in Southern Alberta, where I met my first husband, I took some online courses and became a bookkeeper – *which might I add has done well for me, as everyone needs a great bookkeeper even in the network marketing industry.*

We started a family and, you guessed it, I got into another network marketing company, this time home parties and trade shows where I had to have stock to sell. These were truly brutal times; going into people's homes night after night, trade shows on the weekends, on the phone constantly trying to make sales, writing up orders, packaging, and delivering orders. From makeup to children's clothing sales, I kept moving, growing, and surviving making an extra income for the family. In retrospect, I needed to learn how to balance home life and the industry. Luckily, I have done that now.

Now, some people truly love the aspect of network marketing that is all home parties and trade shows. There's nothing wrong with that. It's just not for me, anymore. So, I found an online company I love with products that are congruent with my lifestyle and requirements. Additionally, their dual sided compensation plan allows me to grow both with customers and with a team (only if one chooses to).

So back to my story .... Moving yet again, this time to Northern Alberta, marrying a second time, I went back into the corporate world. I worked for several years, while always looking for an opportunity to serve others in the industry, both their wellbeing and financially. I didn't get back into the network marketing industry until November 2018, this time all online. Loved it! I was growing and teaching those who are coachable and teachable to achieve the same success I was experiencing.

Stinkin' Thinkin' and Limiting Beliefs

So, let's talk about limiting beliefs for a minute – you know the ones. They haunt you every day – like little tormenting devils sitting on your shoulder – seeing the fat girl in the DAMN mirror, seeing the failures that you have had, seeing the tears you have cried and anger you have had over losses.

YOU, my dear, are limiting your own well-being by believing that DAMN mirror because YOU are capable of anything. Your subconscious mind does not know the difference between the truth and an untruth. So, when you say things like, I am not worthy of great wealth, or I am not worthy of success… Well, your subconscious mind says, "ok, then I guess you are not" and goes with it, bringing in more doubts and worry.

If you train, and I mean *truly take control* and train your subconscious mind to BELIEVE and KNOW your wants and desires to be; wealthy, successful, healthy, and in love with life - then you will be! However, it takes training, devotion, and developing *everyday* towards a better YOU.

The same holds true in the network marketing business. You MUST develop, grow, and consistently be visible on your social platform, in your groups, and with your peers and mentors. If you want to *level up*, seek out and continue to be involved with those whom you want to emulate, gathering gold nuggets of wisdom from those around you. Stay around the people you want to be like, to have the possessions they have, to have the wealth and influence they have. This will grow your mind, bank account, and influence in your circle.

How do we *train our mind*?

Practice gratitude every day – every morning, write down three things you are grateful for; three affirmations to train your brain to turn to the positive:

1. I am worthy of great things
2. I am happy and loved
3. I am beautiful

At the end of the day, write down three wins from the day, they can be anything from big wins or events to the smallest win of that day. Write this on a blue index card with blue ink. I know, you're thinking quirky …! Trust me, if Bob Proctor tells me to do this, I'm all in! Yes, he did!

1. I connected with 10 people today
2. I felt happy and clearly could hear that in my conversations today
3. I went over what went well today, what could be improved on and what I should ditch

Know that you are enough

You CAN do this thing called Network Marketing. You are the only person holding you back.

That *DAMN* mirror – THROW it out – like literally take it off the wall, walk out the door and throw it in the dumpster declaring – I NO LONGER SERVE THE OLD SELF. I DECLARE I AM WORTHY! You will feel uplifted, a weight off your shoulders, believe me.

Get a new mirror – plaster it with new beliefs. Write out your gratitude daily – write out your new positive affirmations daily and WIN!

Practical steps to take every single day

Three things that are practical steps to take in your daily action for Network Marketing:

1. Show up consistently – daily posts on social media, in groups, on your main page, in your friend's feeds – but just SHOW UP

2. Ask the question – "Would you be open to taking a look at my products or opportunity" DAILY –with at least 5 people – you won't know if you don't ask

3. Add new friends – and I'm not talking just any random person –do some homework; friend people whom you would want in your circle as clients or business partners

Take a*ction*!

Other things that affect your network marketing business, are performing IPA's (Income Producing Activities). Posting on social media is **not** an IPA. The conversations that are developed from posting on social media, however, are IPAs. The follow-ups you do daily are IPAs. Learn to follow up with 5, 10, to 20 people daily. If you want to grow, this is a daily ritual.

Get out of your own way and ask the open question to everyone. How many friends do you have on your social media channels? Have you asked every one of them? I would bet that you have only asked maybe 5-8% of them. It's rare that I get anyone saying that they have actually reached out to 10% - very rare. So, what is stopping you from asking them? There are those limiting beliefs again OR you are placing your own perception of their thoughts about your business or products in the way of asking them. What I mean is this – you think "oh they will think it's too expensive", "oh they wouldn't want to do this, they are too busy"; "they won't like the products because they already use ...." Do you follow?

STOP doing this – they might say no, but remember, 'no' means 'not right now'. It doesn't mean they will stop watching you or following you. I've had people watch me for over two years, finally reach back out to me and say, ok tell me what it is and what you are doing. THEY are watching *you*!

I highly suggest going through your friends list once a week, take an hour and start at A (do one letter every week or every day if you want to grow fast) – go through and check out their profiles, see if they are active. If they are, comment on three of their posts, compliment them genuinely, for three days, then send them a private message and see if you get a response. If you don't, don't just write them off, but put them on a list to follow up in three months. Follow up!

What I have found is that doing birthday greetings every day is truly a fantastic way of lifting up your friends– find your list of friend's birthdays and send a genuine greeting – usually by voice is the best. Those who respond in Messenger, always reply and when ending your response, end it with a question so they feel the need to respond back. Keep the conversation going. Say something like – "so what's keeping you busy these days?" They in turn will ask you – and bingo – there's your cue that you can tell them. But don't dwell on it, circle around and take it back to them. Something like, "thanks for asking, I'm on a health and wellness journey. So, tell me, Lisa, are you on one too?" People rarely say no to this as they don't want to admit that they are not watching their health more closely. They'll now be watching you more closely, online to see exactly what it is you are doing.

Have contests and giveaways. I love giving away free products and One on One leadership sessions with my DMO (daily method of operation) sheet. Giveaways and contests then lead to referral posts which friends will gladly post on their social media for a chance at some free product and product credits. You are then getting into a totally new circle of their friends and their friend's friends. The snowball effect begins and your inbox will explode with conversations. Remember the conversations you have to have? IPAs – YES, you are in the business of connecting with people!

Swap posts with other network marketers. Curiosity posting, otherwise known as attraction marketing, is the best way to draw in your audience. They want to know what you are doing since your skin is glowing in that picture, or how you are losing weight, or how that car shines up so well. They want to know how you could afford that new motorhome or vehicle. They want to know how you can spend so much time at the beach or out with you kids at the park. People are curious beings.

Some of the most fun I've ever had is with engagement posts. For example – Would you rather eat ice cream or pudding? What is the most interesting or weird food you have ever eaten? People want to tell you and so they engage in comments, you engage back and then get into their inbox and have those conversations. Again, it goes back to conversations ....

Be authentic, be genuine, be open with your own struggles. Show your face – show your attitude – show your true life not a glossy picture of someone you are not. People want the real thing, not an imposter. People need to know, like and trust you before they will ever buy from you or join you in business. Did you know it now takes 8 to 12 exposures to your products or business before they will trust you?

Show your life, show your wins and your failures, be true to yourself with your own goal. If you only spend an hour a day on your business of network marketing, are you going to make six figures this year? Maybe, if you are very strategic with your time, no scrolling, just doing IPAs for that hour. If you can up that to two one-hour time periods you will have more success and if you can increase it to three one-hour time periods, even more success. You get back what you put into it.

Be a leader who cares and authentically helps your team. Leaders are seeders of information. A leader encourages, cheers on their team, shouts them out on the team page, acknowledges the smallest win. You want to be the leader that they will approach. You want your team to be knowledgeable about the tools and systems that are in place – they need to know where to find things so that they are not reliant on you as a leader but can come to you if there are major problems.

Don't entertain drama within your organization – nip it, immediately. There is no room for drama and it will lead to the demise of your team. Someone with negativity can ruin the reputation of your whole team, and you as the leader. Entertain instead; team spirit, team sharing of ideas, team calls, but have one on one with the runners on your team. You will know them – they will be like you and won't stop until they reach their goal.

One of the biggest learning curves I have had is becoming a leader who can bring fun into the team environment. It's a beautiful thing to be able to learn as you earn, chose your own hours, learn together and have fun doing it.

So, finally, I'm going to tell you to have some FUN in this business. It's your business, not a hobby! Take the tasks you must do seriously but allow some time for fun and creativity. Allow some fun to take place in order to truly enjoy what you are doing – you are in the service of serving others. Don't forget what your purpose truly is.

Back to the mirror – the new mirror!

NOW go look in that **new mirror**, say loud and proud – **I AM WORTHY, I AM GRATEFUL AND I AM A LEADER.**

Chandra lives on an acreage in Northern Alberta, Canada. Chandra is a grandma to 12 grandchildren, mother to three grown adult children. She comes from a background of farming in her younger years, so she knows the meaning of hard work. Chandra is a versatile individual who has found success in the automotive industry, bookkeeping, and retail for many years. Hobbies include reading, cross-stitch and scrapbooking.

She has been in Network Marketing since Nov 2018. Her passion is to help others get their health back or keep their health continuing into the golden years. She is a leader who brings fun and creativity into the industry.

NATALIE FOELLER

"Don't tell me what works, tell me what duplicates."

NATALIE FOELLER

I wasn't raised in a business minded family. My parents were teachers who frequently reminded us of the benefits of a pension plan. We were encouraged to go to University and choose our education based on the likelihood of finding a good professional job. My brother became an engineer and I became a nurse. So far so good….we were on the right path. My parents seemed to have done it right. They loved teaching and their schedule was great for raising a family. They were off summers, Christmas, March break. They taught at the college level and were usually home by the time my brother and I returned from school. Their choices provided a great life growing up.

It didn't take long in my new "professional" career as a Public Health Nurse to realize that maybe there was a different path for me. I was now a part of the system. Schedules, meetings, unions, government bureaucracy….endless redundancy. I was also low man on the totem pole so I needed to ensure the more senior nurses had their vacation in place before mine was approved. I did, however, love my job. The only thing I didn't love was the inflexibility of the schedule. Imagine, they wanted me to show up Monday to Friday, 8:30-4:30 every week … month after month. I did this for over ten years.

How I 'fell" into network marketing

During my time working fulltime as a public health nurse, I was accidentally introduced to Network Marketing. I had some health concerns that lead me to visiting a doctor in Toronto. He was a medical doctor who practiced natural medicine. This Hungarian doctor, in just one meeting, completely shifted my paradigm around health. In just one short appointment my entire perspective had grown, and the seeds of curiosity were planted. I bought books on herbal health, I studied holistic approaches like I was earning a degree. I was fascinated, and passionate in a way that years of Nursing School did not germinate. It all made sense to me. I had never thought of my immune system as something I could strengthen or weaken by the habits and choices I made daily. I had never thought about detoxifying and immune building and cellular nutrition and even quite simply that our cells needed to be fueled properly for peak performance. How did I go to University and earn a Bachelors of Science in Nursing and all of this seemed so new? It was incredulous and I was hungry to learn more.

So how did this and network marketing come together? This doctor, in Toronto, Ontario, put me on supplements. Supplements! Quite a few of them in fact. I came home with supplements for myself, my husband and even a couple products for my very young children. Like I said, my entire paradigm had shifted. This made sense to me. What I did not know at the time was that these supplements came from a Network Marketing Company. Heck, I had never heard of terms like multi-level marketing, direct sales and never really knew of home- based business opportunities. I didn't have a good or bad impression. I had nothing. While sharing my experience with my fellow nurses, one of them recognized the products I was purchasing. She mentioned that a doctor in the town just north of us was also recommending them. She told me that I could purchase a "membership" and save a lot of money buying them directly from the company. At this point I had been buying them from this Toronto doctor at full retail for several months. It didn't take me long to get my own account and "accidentally" fall into my first network marketing experience.

Meetings Build Belief

Just days later I learned of a meeting in Toronto on the very same day my husband was to travel there for a business meeting. The author of the "Chicken Soup for the Soul" book series was going to be speaking at this company meeting, along with someone training on the products. I knew I needed to be there. I didn't know why but my gut told me to make this trip. Just as I had had a huge shift after the appointment with this physician; my whole perspective changed when I heard Mark Victor Hansen share his reasoning for choosing to invest his time in a network marketing endeavor. This incredibly successful, well-known author, carved time in his busy week to build a residual income because he believed in the products, the model of duplication and power of this income stream. If he believed it was worth it; I needed to understand this more. He sent us home with a task. He asked that we not go to bed before booking at least five meetings. Find five friends or family who would put a few people together in a room and allow us to share the benefits of the products. He reminded us we won't be good or polished. We had to begin somewhere. "Do it bad, do it bad until you do it good"!

Network Marketing is easier today than ever!

I started in the early nineties. We didn't have skype, zoom, social media or facetime and didn't even use the internet or have email yet. Long distance calls were expensive and many of us only made those calls after 6 pm or on the weekend. Building a business meant lots of coffee shop meetings, one on one telephone calls, driving long distances and truthfully making a significant time commitment for the potential of a business. By the way, by the time I went to bed that night I had six meetings scheduled. My mom, my sister-in-law and several friends agreed to help. I don't know what they were really thinking, but I asked for their help, and they were agreeable. I'm not sure they realize how much this launched my entire future. I'm also not sure why I was so willing to go out of my comfort zone. I had no mentor. I knew no one successful in this industry. I had no one to follow. Mark Victor Hansen became my role model. I just reminded myself frequently that it was good enough for him, so it was good enough for me. I made friends in the business. They were on other teams, but they wanted to collaborate. We had no marketing tools, no presentations, no systems. We didn't expect this from the company. We knew if we wanted these things, we needed to create them. We were self-employed after all. Our success was 100% related to our own efforts. I often wonder if we have disabled our true entrepreneurs a bit by giving them too much. Today, when someone joins the team; they are spoon-fed everything. The company provides more tools than one could ever use, the teams create solid systems and we never have to leave the comfort of our pajamas to build a dynasty. It's so much easier today. At no time before, in network marketing history, has the opportunity become so available to the masses. They can simply plug in and go. Building an income no longer requires you to spread yourself thin, leave your family nightly (we used to sell the benefits of a home- based business while spending evenings in everyone else's home) or wonder if you have enough financial resources to adequately get started. Communication is essentially free, there really is no long distance anymore and everyone has a phone which is really the only tool required to build a six-figure income. You can literally be earning life-changing income and never ever leave your home. It is an opportunity for everyone. In less than three years doing this very part-time around my full-time nursing career, I had tripled my nursing salary. It was exciting. What was most exciting was knowing that there was no ceiling to my earnings. I was the architect of my business and ultimately my paycheck. I still lay awake at night in deep gratitude.

Hard to believe I began in this industry 28 years ago. I was a young mom with two kids under four and stepchildren who were teenagers, a full-time job and we lived thirty minutes outside the city. My husband was a partner in an accounting firm and worked very long hours. We did not have any extra time. Our plate was full, but our dreams for our future were lit. We both agreed that there had to be more. We made great money, but our careers meant limited vacation time and limited flexibility. We could never be the home that had both parents there when our kids finished school, like my parents. We would never have summers off like my parents. I wanted that and so much more. There had to be more flexibility and freedom. We both knew the sacrifices being made in the short term were destined to pay off in the long run. We understood this and enthusiastically committed. We attended everything. We made arrangements for our kids and travelled to every important event and convention. We were all in and knew our success and the success of our team required it. There were sacrifices. Plenty of sacrifices. But the rewards were plentiful. Only five years after starting down this journey we both retired from our professional careers. I gave up the security of my pension and left a job I did love. My husband sold his practice, and we were now full-time networkers with young children, then only 7 and 9. In truth our kids today really have no memory of us working outside the home. We were always there and sometimes joke they were jealous of the kids whose parents were working as they got to be home alone.

When I look back on the "seasons' of my career it's interesting to plot the evolution of my growth. I wouldn't admit I was in network marketing. I was an "herbal consultant", a "health coach" or an "alternative practitioner". The term multi-level marketing made me squeamish. That was not who I was. I didn't do that kind of business. It was perpetuated by a ten-year career with a company that liked to say they weren't a network marketing company. They'd say they did direct to consumer marketing. I had enough experience to know it was the same thing but many in the company truly convinced themselves they were different. This also made me shy away from truly sharing the gifts of network marketing. I was not contributing to raising the image and reputation of this amazing profession. I was clearly successful. I had a strong six-figure income, a car allowance, and paid trips for years before I ever admitted I was a Professional Network Marketer.

Back to Belief Building...

What happened that made me change this perspective? Back to building belief and attending meetings! I decided to invest and attend courses for professional networkers. Not company-driven trainings, but industry trainings. I flew to Dallas, Las Vegas, and to Los Angeles ... I wanted to be with other top earners. I met amazing men and women who proudly represented our field. They believed to their core they were part of the best industry in the world. They were from a variety of backgrounds which included doctors, lawyers, business people, home makers, engineers and laborers. They had different ethnic backgrounds, were different religions, spoke many languages, from many countries and had no obvious common link, but one very big common denominator. **They believed**. They believed in their company, their product, their compensation plan, the profession, and most importantly, in themselves. They were committed. They were proud. They knew that what they had was the best. They were changing the course of their lives, their family's life, and the lives of thousands they impacted. I finally got it. I was that change agent. I did impact thousands. I could make a difference in a way that my nursing career did not allow. But I had to be as proud of this profession as I was to say I was a nurse. I had to ensure that my conviction was stronger than anyone's skepticism. I had to feel that in every cell of my body. Being around my peers and hearing how they spoke fueled me with the same confidence. I was so busy mentoring and leading my team; I did not take the time to raise my own lid of leadership. I needed to be around success outside of my company leadership. Social proof grows belief exponentially and sitting at events with hundreds of other six-figure income earners cemented my belief that this truly is the best industry in the world. I finally understood why getting our teammates to conventions, leadership summits, and team building activities was paramount. They needed the same opportunity to have their cups filled with belief. This took me almost twenty years to learn.

A lot has happened during my tenure in Network Marketing. I've lost several friends to illness, I've endured the obstacles of changing companies and my husband passed away unexpectedly on the same month I made the highest rank held in Canada by my company (at the time). A bittersweet month. What never dimmed was my passion for my work. If anything, loss has reminded me how very fortunate I have been to have my business be this career. When I needed time to grieve, my leaders were there. The systems were in place so the team was not impacted by my temporary absence. All the things we preached about residual income was true. Losing my husband at the age of fifty could have put me in a very different position. I could have had a great deal more to deal with but instead I had a team who encouraged me to take as much time as I needed. They reminded me they were equipped and did not need me. I had done my job and the team thrived without me.

Now I look back to my almost thirty years and wonder what life would have been like had I not had those paradigm shifts when I was in my 30's. The small decision to visit this doctor I had heard about, to attend the meeting I had read about, or to pursue my business when I had no mentors guiding me. The small decisions to take a chance opened doors of opportunity that could have been missed. If you are wondering if this industry is for you, don't hesitate any longer. Nothing is lost in the journey of experience. This profession welcomes everyone with open arms, and the very nature of our industry is to hook arms with you until you reach your desired level of success. Nowhere else will have you have such a team of supporters invested in your success. It changed my life, and it can change yours too.

Natalie Foeller is a mother and step-mother to 4 adult children. A grandmother to a ten-year-old granddaughter, and another granddaughter on the way. Natalie splits her year between her home in Peterborough, Ontario (and the summer cottage in Minden, Ontario) and their winter home in Florida. After becoming a widow in 2013 she was fortunate to meet a wonderful man and start building new chapters in her life.

She has trained from stages around the world, but is at her happiest sitting in comfy clothes training from home. Her gift is vision casting and helping to build belief. As a mindset coach impacting thousands, Natalie continues to fill her own cup to ensure she remains relevant.

Believe.

GERALYN SCHULKIND

"I'm younger now than I'll ever be again, so I'm going to Carpe Diem."

GERALYN SCHULKIND

Aloha! Allow me to introduce myself. My name is Geralyn Schulkind and I am approaching my 7th decade on this earth. That's really trippy for me to comprehend. I still feel 30, maybe 40 at the most. Let that be a note to yourself when meeting those who are older than you. Many of us are still feeling perky and spry and that's the kind of people you want to attract anyway!

So, let's rewind and I will start at the beginning. I am the oldest girl, the 5th child of 11 children, one mom, one dad. I had 8 brothers and 2 sisters. That alone makes one pretty tough growing up with 4 older brothers. This all helped me learn how to deal with a lot of personalities, which is pretty helpful when building your dream team. It also helped me learn how to ignore insults, my brothers could be pretty mean at times! These are all attributes needed to build a successful life and business. Life was simple back then before computers! No cell phones, all phones were attached to cords and either on the wall or on a table.

Now, when I was 16, my closest brother Nicky was 18. On July 12, 1969 he was with his best buddy and they were drag racing, the car hit a telephone poll, Nicky flew through the windshield. This was the night my world stood still. He was in a coma for 3 days, the emergency room and the waiting room was packed full of friends and family, all of us crying and praying. On July 15th my brother took his last breath. I felt like the air was taken out of me too. Life was different after that. Christmas holidays were extremely painful for our family. Looking for comfort with my sweetheart, I got pregnant. My mom encouraged me to get married or give my baby up for adoption. What was I going to do? Well, I graduated high school at 17, got married and gave birth all in 1970. After 2 years, I got divorced and somewhat stumbled through life for awhile. I went back with another high school boyfriend. He wasn't such a good choice. I was blessed with another beautiful daughter with him. So here I was, 22 years old with 2 daughters and an unstable relationship. I was able to start college, get on welfare and keep my girls close. Then on June 30, 1976 I got a call from my brother Pete telling me my mother and niece had drowned. The world halted once more and my mind went into a spin. While still spinning, on May 8th, the first Mother's Day after mom died, my brother called me again. I was thinking he was calling to check on me to see how I am doing on the first Mother's Day after our mom died. Well, no, he was calling to tell me dad died.

Big sigh.

FAST FORWARD.

Right now, I am sitting in first class on a plane and writing this to you. Thankful, grateful, blessed. I am pondering what it is that I can share with you to help you succeed? Well, I'm still thinking I need to take you on my life's journey, not in too much detail, but enough to let you see you can overcome life's challenges and build the life you've always dreamed of, I promise you can.

So just like that I am an orphan at age 23, both mom and dad gone. Sigh. My parents and I were just rebuilding our relationship because they had not been happy with my choice of boyfriends. This was 1976, the era of "Remember the Titans", a great movie in my opinion, and my second daughter's dad was black. Here I am, 2 beautiful daughters, one vanilla and one chocolate. The odds were stacked against me that I would be able to be a success.

Have you ever heard of the author, Og Mandino? I highly recommend you read his books. I'm very thankful a teacher in junior high school had us read his book <u>The Greatest Salesman</u> as an assignment. You see, I learned good habits are the key to success. It taught me to keep persevering. It taught me that our uniqueness is a gift. Also, it taught me time is precious and I can control my emotions through utilizing positive actions.

Another favorite author is Zig Ziglar. He once said; "Desire is the catalyst that enables a person with average ability to compete and WIN against others with more natural talent." There are many life- changing quotes for which he's famous. Here's another; "You can have everything in life you want, if you will help other people get what they want."

Basically, you can achieve what you want in life if you have the above. Remember that please.

Let's think now hmmm. So, I forgot to mention I was born in Washington, DC and was living in Minneapolis, because my boyfriend had a scholarship to the University of Minnesota at this time. I went to the community college while I was there and I was on welfare! So, when both of my parents died when I was far away, I figured it was time to go home again. Those Minnesota winters were cruel anyway! I broke up with my second daughter's dad when he started to get volatile as I did not want my girls growing up in that environment, and now I was back where I was born. I had to figure out how to support my girls. I got an apartment and a job. I seriously did walk at least three miles every week day. First mile to drop my oldest to her school bus stop, then another half mile to my second daughter's child care. Then another mile or so to the bus then to the subway then another few blocks to my job at the US Chamber of Commerce across from the White House. That was interesting and fun, and I met some fabulous people. Then the summer came and I started freaking out about child care and WHO would be raising MY GIRLS! You know, I figured they were pretty OK in school with their teachers, but at this time during summer vacation, I'm thinking this is going to be their WHOLE waking lives! So, I start talking, thinking, searching, and praying for answers. I wanted to be with my girls most of the time. It was then I discovered waitressing. My sister-in-law told me about a restaurant near my place where she used to work. She said it was frequented by many of the area's business owners and that it could be a stepping stone to a career. Which it was! Thankful, grateful, blessed! So, when the girls went back to school, I started with a printing company as a sales rep. They gave me a small salary and commission. And I still worked the restaurant! Yes, two jobs, two daughters, too fun. Building a future. Dreaming big. I wanted to create a life for my girls that they could be proud of and I wanted them to be proud of me. I prayed.

So, our childhood home was left to the 10 of us children who were still alive. My brother bought us out and with that, I got $8000 that I used to purchase my first home! Soon after I was driving a company car paid for by my printing company and had my girls in private school. Success!! I beat the odds!!

Fast forward again, I meet my future husband at a Halloween party. We date, fall in love and much to his parent's chagrin, I got engaged to their only son, the doctor. I was his parent's nightmare. I'm a divorcée, and the mom of 2 girls, Ebony and Ivory. So yeah, they forbid our marriage, go figure!

Well, we got married anyway. Now almost 35 years later, we're still figuring out this thing called marriage! We were blessed with a son hoping to carry on the family name, but our amazing son, now 32, has Down's syndrome. Another twist in my life! Right after Nate was born, my then 15-year-old daughter, who is half black and half white is holding Nate and looking at him with a strange look on her face. I said to her "what are you thinking? Who will have a tougher life, you or Nate?" Well, the answer to that question was a punch. Although it seemed insurmountable at first, it turned out to be a huge blessing. To be continued in the next chapter!

So, where does Network marketing come into the picture? Well, when I was at my first apartment in Maryland, a sweet waitress friend introduced me to a company. It really was the first time I heard of multi-level marketing. I thought the concept was MARVELOUS! Teamwork always makes the dream work. I loved sports and teams and knew how important that is. But the timing wasn't right for me. I said no, but imagine if I'd said yes to her in 1979 and started building a business then!

I have tried a few different companies in the past and found my heart and home now for the last ten years. I'm working with exciting, energetic and accomplished people.

Bottom line folks, life does throw us some punches. And we can throw them right back! With a good attitude, determination, and the deep desire to succeed you can do it! Do what? Most anything you put your mind to. I believe in you!

With my business, I've been able to make my sixties the most fun decade of my life! Traveling the world and calling it work!! Going to countries where I did not know the language and yet learning how to effectively communicate. Meeting wonderful and like-minded people everywhere all around the world. People who want to make people better, to give them hope and purpose, helping them dream again!

Let's get your party started! Don't hesitate! Jump in!

Dream without fear and

love without limits.

BRENDA PEARCE

"All health is CELL health."

BRENDA PEARCE

A Wellness Shift - It is Time

Why is it that in this day of advancing technology we are sicker now than ever before?

That was the question that plagued me during my years as a working frontline RN. I worked for nearly 40 years and have seen so much in the healthcare world. During my nursing career, I have literally touched thousands of lives and been a part of the most personal and vulnerable times in a person's life. I have seen compassionate care and brilliant breakthroughs along with the effects of simply holding someone's hand to ease the fear and pain.

It was one day, a few years ago that changed how I looked at wellness and healthcare forever. The first part of my career, I thought that wellness was based on your family medical history. That unless it came from a physician's prescription pad, procedure, or pill, there wasn't anything that could be done to facilitate health and wellness.

I remember the day that changed!

I had been co-producing integrative wellness events throughout my region. I was introduced to and learning so much about ways of looking at and taking care of our health and wellness, and the truth is that many diseases can be prevented. In my experience as a nurse, what I now saw was many people creating ownership of their various diseases i.e. "My arthritis is acting up", or "My breathing difficulties", or "My bad heart". I have learned a few things about this ownership of disease. Firstly, when you own it, you become it. Secondly, you give your ownership of your health outcomes over to someone who can manage it. Thirdly, many people forget that the body is an amazing thing, that with proper nutrition, and self-care of body, mind and spirit, you can change outcomes.

I remember the day when this all clicked.

Having been a part of the health care system for decades, I knew something had to change. I wanted to change. I wanted to be a part of the change. At an event I attended, I had the pleasure of meeting an incredible woman who was talking about a product that was showing amazing results. I had to hear the message several times before it finally sank in. This product could help me. Once I saw the value of what this product could bring to me, I purchased without hesitation.

Ironically, even though my only intention was to use this product for myself, the business found me. People started to notice a real change in how I was feeling and living. Between them approaching me, and my not being able to stay quiet about how healthy I was becoming, my business started exploding. My sponsor took me by the hand and helped me to understand the simple process to help my customers and teammates have success as well. The system was so easy to duplicate, that I now do this for my team on my own.

Providing support is the cornerstone for any successful business.

I now see a legacy that I have created, not only for myself and my family, but also for my team members.

I have now retired from my nursing career, not because I no longer want to serve people, but because I can now share with people how to have a better quality of life, including time and financial freedom.

It is my mission, my vision, and passion to spread this news and help as many people as possible.

I tried various network marketing businesses through the years and had various degrees of success. I always loved the products and enjoyed the networking. I am very grateful that I never gave up on the industry. It has changed my life.

My suggestions for success in the MLM industry are:

- Be open minded to opportunity
- Never give up looking for the right fit in the industry

- Remember: Change is possible

Brenda Pearce RN (Non-Practicing) is known as the Empowered Nurse. She is an author, podcaster, TV Show Producer/Host of Oxford Empowered TV on the Rogers TV Network. She is an educator in integrative wellness.

Brenda lives in a small town in Ontario, Canada.

The body is an amazing thing, that with proper nutrition, and self-care of body, mind and spirit, you can change outcomes.

KATE MOIR

"A goal is a dream with a deadline." - Napoleon Hill.

KATE MOIR

Let me start off by saying there isn't much different between you and me. If you have 5 minutes to spare throughout your day, you can make an income from your phone or laptop with this industry. My mission is to help entrepreneurs get off the hamster wheel and make an income throughout the pockets of their day, such as while they wait to pick up the kids from school or while they wait in line at the coffee shop. I truly believe this industry is changing lives and can change yours too if you are consistent and authentic.

You see, I am a wife, a mom, and a mentor with a passion for helping mom bosses get off the hamster wheel so they have more time for the things they love most. I am grateful for this opportunity to share my story and tips with you here so you can stop the "overwhelm" and build the life of your dreams!

You see, I failed in network marketing TWICE before I had kids. I failed because I lacked commitment to the business model. I failed because I stopped taking action and lacked clear goals. I failed because I gave up before I even gave this industry a chance.

Things almost ended up being the same with my third company because I knew the system: buy the kit for a great price, have a party to make the kit back, and quit. Voila! I never dreamed that this little kit would change the trajectory of my life. It was September 2015, I was exhausted, pregnant, and nursing my one-year-old for the 387th day in a row. I needed to find ME again. I needed something that was mine, that was fun, but also guilt free. So, I signed up, then dabbled a bit for a few months.

When I went on maternity leave 6 months later, I had a choice to make: take a break and enjoy being a *girl mom,* or play full out and see where I could take my business while not having to balance *work life* with *mom life*. I chose the latter. When I set a goal, I chase it with an all-in spirit and a can-do attitude.

Within 9 months on maternity leave I had grown my team from 4 to 75 and double promoted. When I returned to work, I doubled my team again in another six months and found myself in the top 1% of the company in all four recognition categories. That meant I was top in recruiting, building leaders, selling, and having strong team sales. With all this success you might think "wow, she must have been living the life!" Instead, I found myself working two full time jobs: my government 9 to 5, and my "side gig", on top of being a wife, mom, and exhausted 32 year old. I weighed more than I did when I was pregnant, was burning the candle from both ends, and was on this hamster wheel.

After too many late nights working double shifts between my two jobs and a panic attack, I was faced with another choice: a successful career as a city planner, an entrepreneur and mentor for my team, or my health. I chose entrepreneurship because I knew that the ceiling was only determined by how big I dreamed versus the pay scale decided by a union and my employer. I would no longer have to ask for permission for time off or have someone shut down my creative spirit. I could work around my husband's 24/7 shifts and be a present mom. I would be able to have the time to take care of me and my health.

It wasn't that simple. Entrepreneurship comes with new challenges that no one really explained. I hope sharing my lessons with you helps you avoid the mistakes I made and remember these three things:

You are worthy of your dreams

You deserve success

You have five minutes or more a day to invest in your future, so don't let another minute slip by

Lesson #1 - Mindset is everything!

Do you know why 98% of network marketers fail? They never believed in themselves, their product, or their company. Seriously.

Before you read any further, I want you to evaluate your current state of belief in:

- Yourself and your ability to succeed. Is it less than 100%? You need to believe in your capacity and your dreams. Anyone can do this industry if they believe in their ability to lean in and give it a solid chance.
-
- Your product. You have to love your product or service and share it without any "Cole's Notes" or hesitation. This business is more than a paycheque, and people can sense your authenticity.
-
- Your company. If you aren't aligned with their vision, mission, or question their ethics or practices, this is a big red flag. It can be hard to grow with a company with whom you don't align or see the big future.

Ok, now that we have done that quick evaluation, where are you at? If you are at 100% in all three - WOW - you are in PRIME position for thriving! If not, don't stress! Most are not 100% in all three, but know that you can change that! Keep your answers in your mind while you read on and consider if there are things you can do to increase your belief so that you can be as close to 100% in all three questions above.

So, you may be thinking, wow, must be nice to be Kate and have 100% belief in herself, her company and her product. I couldn't because of (insert any common excuse here). STOP THAT stinking thinking. Seriously. That is the exact OPPOSITE mindset you want to have. That thinking is going to get you no further than where you were yesterday or last month or last year or…you get the idea. Instead, I want you to throw out every negative thought you have about this industry and just visualize for a moment.

One year from now where are you? Who are you with? What is different in your life? You could get super specific and think about this exact day one year from now.

What time do you wake up at?

Where are you waking up?

Who is beside you?

What does your day entail?

How do you feel?

How much money is in your bank account?

A year ago, I dreamed of waking up on my own accord, no alarm, no set schedule. I could say "yes" to that adventure with my husband and the kids and we had enough money in the bank to pay for it. I'm happy to say that is exactly my life now! I am writing this chapter from the passenger seat of our dream Yukon Denali XL as we drive back from a week-long road trip from seeing family and friends. This was after I just got back from Punta Cana for a week with my mom and a 12-day trip with my kids and husband to Mexico. That was three trips back-to-back without having to ask for permission for days off or using up my vacation time. The ability to work an hour a day on the road saying yes to more adventure with my loved ones. This life wasn't built over night but was a result of having the mindset that I could and would build a laptop lifestyle.

Six years ago, I couldn't say that. I was the Chief Administrative Officer of a municipality, working sixty plus hours a week, living paycheque to paycheque. I was the last person people would share the opportunity with because I was "successful" and "busy". What they didn't know was I missed having fun, guilt free time with friends and my family. Also, I was managing a five million dollar municipal budget, but because of my age and experience, I was at the lowest pay scale for my profession. I felt undervalued. I was bored. I wanted more. I deserved more!

Maybe you have felt that same way or know someone who feels unfulfilled, counting down the decades until retirement. The only difference between them and me, is I took action and did something about my situation. I knew life didn't have to be this way.

It wasn't all sunshine and rainbows. There were moments of loneliness. There were moments of overwhelm. There were moments of what the f*ck am I doing? There were breakdowns and moments where I was immobilized. There were high moments and low moments. The best part is that, through the ups and downs, I was able to help others like you and me adapt and overcome. That is the mindset I lead with every day - what impact can I make while moving forward towards reaching my goals?

Lesson #2 - Get focused with your goals

Buckle up as I am going to help you grow each season, faster than you ever had before without going backward. Seriously, if I could talk about one thing and one thing only, it is goal setting.

I have always set goals. When I was in high school, I wanted to graduate early so I could save money for college. When I was in college, I wanted to have a job before I graduated. When I was in my twenties, I said I would be a boss, wife and mom before I was thirty. In all of these scenarios I achieved my goals! Why? I visualized it. I made a plan. I took action. Now I know that things like marriage and kids aren't completely in one's control, but the principal is that a goal is a dream with a deadline.

So, in my business I approached it the same way. I wanted to be a director in time for my first conference nine months later. I determined what I needed to do and took a season to do just that. In most companies, you can rank up in ninety days or less if you are willing to dive in.

I then wanted to grow my business to earn the top 1% of the company in a year. I broke it down into seasons and tackled sales one season, recruiting another, then promoting leaders the next. This systematic goal setting and focus allowed me to not feel overwhelmed.

There are two things I want to share with you about goal setting basics:

First - each season pick your focus. You can't grow in all areas all at once. So, if you aren't selling over $2,000.00 a month yet in your business, start there. Build your success before tackling anything else. Then if you are rocking a solid sales business, focus on growing your team. Ask all your customers if they have thought about doing what you do, or ask for referrals, etc.

Once you have a team launching their businesses, focus on helping your teammates sponsor and build their own teams. Rinse and repeat. You will be running a 100+ team in no time by duplicating without losing your hair!

The second thing about goal setting is having a clear number in mind. My friend explained it perfectly to me! First, grab your numbers from the past three months:

- What's your lowest? That's your happy goal!
- What's your average? That's your super happy goal!
- What's your best? That's your rock-star goal!

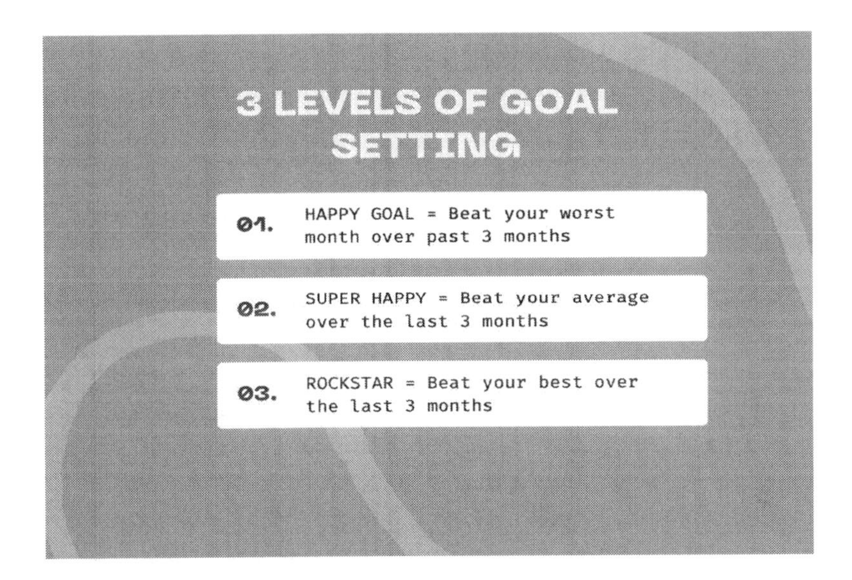

That is your monthly goal moving forward! Never dip below your lowest, then you are at least maintaining! Beat your average to grow! Beat your best to explode! Keeping it simple is key!

Going back over one year is too long and has too many variables, but each season, if you maintain at least, you aren't moving backward! P.S. You can apply this to sales, parties, recruits, team sales, promotions, etc.

Another way to track your progress is tracking your numbers. My up-line suggested tracking numbers at minimum the 7th, 14th, 21st, and 28th of each month! Daily if you are running for a goal! This allows you to see if you are on track or need to kick it up a notch with your income producing activities.

Whatever you do, numbers don't lie and can tell you what's happening in your business so you can continue to grow.

Lesson #3 - Consistency is key

Remember, when I launched my business, I was working a full-time job, commuting an hour to work, and pregnant with a one-year-old running around. Sleep was over rated. I didn't have an up-line to lean on. I had me, myself and I, with a baby on the way.

This is where I learned to maximize the five minutes throughout my day. I would post before work. I would reply to comments on my morning coffee break. I would do follow up messages while I ate my lunch. I would reply to messages before bed. I deleted games off my phone and spent the time most people waste scrolling social media to work my business. If I had an idea or saw something, I shared it immediately. I didn't second guess or question whether anyone else would benefit from it. If I found it useful or it made me smile, I shared it. Progress over perfection, remember? That was my mantra. Day in, day out, I made progress one step forward.

Now, at times this meant I was "throwing spaghetti to the wall". I was hoping something would stick. I was probably posting too much, too random without a thought of if this was "on brand", but it was progress. In hindsight, I should have proof-read my posts more and let my team learn to fish vs feeding them, but it resulted in us all growing together.

So today, think about your daily method of operation. What do you do every day that is income producing? Here is my list:

5 MIN TASKS EACH DAY

Today is: ....

Gratitude of the day:

5 minute tasks to grow influence	5 minute tasks for income producing
value added post	curiosity post
send private birthday messages	review / testimony post
comment on 10 stories / reels / posts	follow up with at least 5 people you talked to recently
follow 10 new people from likeminded groups	expose 5 to your product/offer
ask for the referral / booking	follow up with 5 customers
connect with those currently online	share opportunity video to at least 1 person

Take time each night to reflect on your day and set your intentions for tomorrow!

You see, there are activities that provide value and then there are things that produce income. Value is always fun but not necessarily going to produce income. You can't have a store that isn't open and isn't selling anything. Imagine if your favourite store never shared a promo, didn't have an inventory list or a location to go visit?

Your business is the same way. You are open 24/7 if you have a website, but people won't know that unless they know the website address! Your friends won't know if they want to take a look if you aren't sharing what you have in stock and what problem your product solves. Oh, and people love to buy what others are loving. Reviews provide that FOMO (fear of missing out) and sales create a sense of urgency. These are just the basics so think about your social media as your online store and you are the biggest asset. So, add value, have fun, and share what you are enjoying.

It also cannot be all business or then you are that store that is super spammy that people block or unsubscribe. You want to be the store that is so intriguing and interesting that people are always wanting to see what's new. They are telling their friends about you. They are counting down to your new releases and your website is bookmarked!

These take time but if every day you did even a couple activities from both columns above, you will grow. If taking daily action is new to you, remember adjust your actions to your goals and keep your dreams in mind. The future is yours to build with your business!

My number one piece of advice to have success in this business:

Get serious and dream bigger instead of just treating it like a hobby. Lean into your company's systems but have the courage to be yourself every step of the way. People want to buy from or join with someone they like, know, and trust. Allow them to do just that by getting loud and being present and authentically you on social media.

About Kate Moir

A wife, mom, and mentor that coaches mom bosses to get off the hamster wheel and reclaim their time back through 5 minute daily actions they can do in the pockets of their day. She is an upper-level leader that has personally sponsored over 400 people in her 7-year career as a network marketer. Kate lives a laptop lifestyle working from wherever the next adventure takes her and her family. She lives her dream life on an acreage in Minnedosa, Manitoba, and is often seen sipping coffee or coaching others while walking around town.

Get serious and dream bigger instead of just treating it like a hobby.

JANICE PORTER

"Don't build links ... Build Relationships!"

JANICE PORTER

I always knew I wanted to be my own boss … I just didn't know what that would look like.

Teaching was my first profession – and I loved it. What nobody told me was that I had to deal

with politics, bureaucracy and people who were so set in their ways that it was a constant downer. I took some time off for health reasons and began to see that perhaps teaching school wasn't going to be IT forever. When it was time to go back to work, I couldn't do it – and as luck would have it (there really are no accidents, in my opinion), I was given the opportunity to do some corporate training. My next adventure, in the world of "adult education" began.

I was one step closer to being my own boss and parlayed a contract position into a pretty steady 18-year gig. Then it all came crashing down in the early 2000s as the economy changed and contract employees were being squeezed out. No job, no pension, no gold watch.

Now what?

There was no chance I was going to be an employee with a 9 – 5 routine – perish the thought.

I had 2 daughters and a busy "mom" schedule that included dance and piano, for one daughter and three sports for the other. The reality was I needed to work to help pay for all those activities, but I also needed the flexibility to be where I needed to be – cheering on my kids.

But here's the problem – I didn't know a thing about business – how to start one, how to run one, and how to finance one. I discovered that I didn't qualify for government assistance to go and learn how to become a business owner – except for a 2-week program that gave the Cliff/Coles Notes version – just enough information to be dangerous.

I began networking like crazy. Networking was now a thing, and I made sure I got myself out there, meeting people, learning by asking questions, and getting involved at my local Chamber of Commerce so I could see what "small business" was all about. I thought I could set myself up as an independent, corporate and tech trainer in the same industry I had been in. Sounded easy, and I knew my stuff – but I soon realized that no one was going to feed me the work – as the scheduler had in my previous contract position. I had to market myself and get out there.

I also had to keep up with the latest iterations of the equipment I was training on – which was much harder to do on my own. Things didn't go so well.

One of the women I met networking was a true entrepreneur who had a couple of businesses going … I learned lots from her and actually began my next venture by licensing her business – and became a professional organizer, focused on small office, home office clients.

I worked hard to make my skills known at networking events, started doing presentations to

give value and build a client base. I also learned some business acumen from my mentor and business partner. That lasted for a couple of years – and at the same time I started to build my reputation as a master networker – joining several networking organizations and helping to build the local chapters. Being a good networker and connector has really helped me a lot along the way – and, guess what? I was able to train others how to be more successful at that skill too – and get paid for it. Progress!

Somewhere in the middle of all that I was introduced to network marketing. I'm sure I was lured once to a secret meeting in someone's living room that had a stranger up at the front of the room with a flip chart drawing Xs and Os. The dark ages of MLM for sure. That didn't work for me. But I seemed to be drawn to the next one and the next one as I was curious and always seeking another way to make extra money.

I committed to my first real network marketing company because a friend talked me into it. We were some of the first in Canada to be involved – the problem was, we were the blind leading the blind and had no idea what we were doing. I gave it a good shot, and quickly found out that their main products were not my thing.

You'd think that would be enough – but I did it again – this time it was a brand-new company that had a health drink which I actually enjoyed taking and was doing some good for me – the problem was that it was very expensive, and I didn't know how to sell it. It wasn't a natural fit for me and I was uncomfortable. People all around me were finding success and it eluded me … again.

They say 3rd time is the charm, and while I was treading water with my second company I was introduced to my present company – which I have now been with since 2008. I finally found a company that had products and services that I could totally identify with and share with others. At first, I said – NO MORE network marketing for me – I will just be a customer and use the products. But being a natural networker, I started telling others about it – a sign that I saw value in the product – and then I realized that I could get mine paid for if I became an affiliate.

The journey still wasn't easy, but this time I felt "at home" and comfortable with the products. That was a start. The person who brought me into this company was there to support me as needed and had my back. Now I began to really learn about the industry.

I really believe that network marketing is continuous lessons in personal development, as you are always being challenged to push yourself and see what you are made of.

One of those lessons came a couple of years in with this company and I was on an incentive trip to Mexico, that I had earned. I was pretty excited as I got to spend time with the big earners and listen to things that they were doing to be successful. I had a huge AHA moment in a class at the event as the presenter was talking about our MLM Blueprint and the importance of belief in the network marketing model. He asked on a scale of 1 – 10 what was our blueprint.

It was then that I realized that mine was not very high – which is why when I presented my products and opportunity to people, I had this pit in my stomach and I received a fair number of objections. Is this a pyramid scheme? Only the top few people make any money, right?

As I began to work through that and believe in the model more and more, I stopped having those objections. My MLM blueprint shot up – no more stomach pains when I was prospecting.

I started to build my confidence and my belief. That was a huge turning point for me.

It is a known fact in the industry that going to live events is important as they can be so impactful. You are "close to the fire" as they say, and it can be very motivating. I love going

to events and they always include a celebration section where those who have reached certain levels in their business, are rewarded as they walk across the stage. In my company you had to reach a mid-level status to be able to stand on the stage and cheer on the newer people's accomplishments. After watching people reach the level of status to be on the stage too many times over the years I finally had had enough! I made a declaration that I was going to be there at the next annual event, whatever it took!

That's when the work really began, as I didn't realize how much discipline and grit it takes to make things happen. It went down to the wire. I had almost reached the goal … just a few last customers needed …. I called in a few favors (which actually taught me another amazing lesson) and reached my goal. The pride and sense of accomplishment I felt was through the roof and did a lot to solidify my belief in this amazing industry.

At the next event, as I walked across the stage I was beaming with such pride and joy!

One of my favorite moments in the industry was being introduced to the work of Jim Rohn. He was one of my first inspiring mentors and I used to listen to his network marketing CD over and over again – especially the parable about sowing and reaping. It just said it all – and that's how I learned the MOST valuable information about not taking things personally. You can't control who is going to come to your meeting, you can't control who is going to buy, you can't control who will leave, you can't control anything other than YOU and your feelings. The sooner you don't take things personally the easier it is to move on and find the people who want what you want.

A huge bonus of being part of the network marketing industry is the people I've met.

By building a business mostly online I have customers and affiliate partners all over the world. By going to company and industry events I've met some of the most amazing, positive, generous people who have become lifelong friends. It's always fun to know that I can work anywhere and that I have connections in so many places as a result of this great industry.

My number one piece of advice to have success in this business is to never give up! As one of my mentors always says – never give up on a bad day! Believe in yourself and you will be surprised where it can take you. This is an industry that allows anyone to reach their dreams as long as they are willing to work for them.

For Janice, it's all about relationships! First and foremost is her family – her husband and two daughters – and most of all her precious little granddaughter. Her passion is working with people who care about people and want to build their businesses through staying connected to others. She trains business professionals to use LinkedIn to attract new clients and new referral partners and then shows them how to implement a tangible touch follow up system with clients, prospects and associates to stay in front of them, while at the same time celebrating and appreciating them on a consistent basis. Janice really values the friendships and business relationships she makes and when she meets someone new is always thinking: "How may I support you?"

Never give up on a bad day!
Believe in yourself and you will
be surprised
where it can take you.

KAREN HEINEMANN

"You will have whatever you believe"

KAREN HEINEMANN

The Road Warrior Life

I spent most of my career as a Road Warrior, commuting to my weekly job via airplane. I was a super busy, 65+ hour a week, 100% on-the-road corporate executive, a simultaneously invigorating and stressful job.

A typical week consisted of waking to an alarm at 3:30AM on a Monday morning allowing enough time to shower, dress, finish packing, grab an Uber or Lyft and get to the airport with just enough time to fly through airport security (it made a big difference to have TSA pre-check. If you can get it, I highly recommend it!) and plop down in my assigned seat on board the airline going to my assigned work destination.

On Friday, it was always a mad rush to the airport as afternoon meetings ran long, the rental car needed to be filled with gas and returned, I had to wait for the bus to the terminal and hope the security line wasn't too long. After all that, on many an occasion, there was a flight delay or worse a cancellation. Would I make it home by 10PM, later, or not at all?

Weekends at home were routine - unpack, do laundry, run a few errands, pay bills, see a couple of friends on Saturday night or brunch on Sunday. Repack, check-in for my flight, set the alarm for 3:30AM and go again.

I loved to travel so it was exciting that my assignments were at unfamiliar locations where I was often set up in a corporate apartment for a minimum of 6 months, but typically longer. While I found enjoyment in my job, it was often very socially limiting. As a Contracted Chief Information Officer and General Manager, I had to walk a fine line and balance the delicate vendor/client relationship. The relationships were friendly but could never become established friendships, at least until I was no longer assigned to that particular contract.

Evenings in the apartment or hotel were spent having dinner, finishing up work to meet deadlines and then drop into bed with my tortoiseshell cat, Chelsea who was an amazing travel companion - she flew more confidently than the million-milers, she relaxed and enjoyed the car rides and found comfort at the corporate apartment or hotel of the week. I was happy to have her with me as she made life on the road more fun and comforting.

Back at home, I missed celebrating birthdays and special events. Friends stopped inviting me to do things because they knew I wasn't available Monday through Friday, and some weekends. Being a road warrior was an isolated lifestyle and often, very lonely.

One week while on the road, I dislocated my wrist and was in great pain as I hurriedly dragged my over-stuffed carry-on suitcase and briefcase through the long corridors of the Denver airport. Sitting in my seat on the plane, I looked through the window at the Rocky Mountains and thought, "What would happen to me if I became unable to travel?" My livelihood depended on being healthy and vital enough to handle the physical and mental demands of the ever-increasing stress of travel and life on the road. A chill ran through my body as I contemplated what would become of me, a single woman with a mortgage, bills, and life expenses. I needed a back-up plan. Maybe even an exit strategy for the future.

Over the next several days, overwhelming anxiety filled me as I imagined losing my ability to travel for work. My mind whirled with thoughts of losing my independence, the inability to pay my bills, and the potential loss of my home. What could I do to prepare should this unfortunate situation come to fruition? I needed to find an opportunity I could lean into, and feel confident that I was ready for whatever might happen.

Multi-Level Marketing, For Me?

I had heard of people who had made a good living in the Multi-level Marketing industry. I had been to "In home parties" where wonderful products such as skincare, clothes, cookware, wine, and more were presented in a relaxed and fun atmosphere. I enjoyed learning about the products being presented and learning about the respective companies and the opportunities they offered, but at the time I believed that just wasn't for me. I had a good job, I didn't need extra income, I certainly did not have any time available for a side-gig, and I didn't know anyone who would want to buy those products from me.

But with a desire for a solution to my dilemma, I began to reflect on those in-home parties and the information I had heard about the income generating opportunities. The thoughts of an MLM were reoccurring and finally it hit me, why not find out more? Perhaps an MLM is just the back-up plan and future exit strategy I need.

I began my professional career as a Federal Government Analyst investigating everything from foreign adoption to strategic weapons systems. I decided to use my investigative and research skills to learn more about MLM companies. Could there be one that was right for me? As I began my search, I discovered there are hundreds of reputable MLM companies selling high quality, often patented merchandise. It became apparent I needed a list of criteria to help narrow down and discover the right company for me. For example, I needed a company that did not require I carry inventory and ship products from home, success had to be based on more than just hosting in-home parties; I didn't want the pressure of quotas, and I had to be able to work the side-gig within the nooks and crannies of my 65+ hour a week corporate job, and I need to be able to work it from anywhere and everywhere.

I was doing my due-diligence and over several months using my list of criteria, I was able to narrow my MLM company selection to 3 companies. My next step was to seek out successful people from each company and interview them; I even flew to Ohio to meet a Representative! I was clear with each representative that I was on a search to find my perfect company, that I would not be joining at the end of the meeting and that I would be getting back with them with my decision.

I was fortunate to have found a company within the three that met my list of criteria, and after a few days of consideration, I joined! I was excited about my decision, relieved that I now had a back-up plan to my corporate life, and was proud of how my due diligence had paid off.

A New Beginning

I joined my new side-gig company with a $500 kit that included products, marketing material, a website and "support." Admittedly, I was nervous. "What have I done?" "Am I crazy to believe I can fit one more responsibility into my schedule?" "What if I don't understand how to do it?" "What will my friends and family think?" "I haven't even tried the products yet, what if they are horrible?" Fear of failure and what others would think of my new venture consumed me. My mindset was not nearly as strong as I had thought. Where was my established level of regular and sustained confidence that had brought me great success as a Corporate Executive? Well, it was too late for all that. I had made a commitment and I was determined to find a way to integrate this new entrepreneurial endeavor into my existing life.

Initially, I decided that my new side-gig would be a hobby, something I would do when I went back to my corporate apartment or hotel to fill the quiet evenings, and with Wi-Fi onboard the plane I could work my side-gig while I flew back and forth to make the flights go by more quickly.

Unexpectedly, I discovered I was really enjoying my new hobby! I had no idea that I would legit fall in love with my new side-gig. I was immediately welcomed and warmly embraced by my new-found colleagues; I started making new friends from all over the country, and the unconditional encouragement and support of one another blew me away! I was drawn to the positive environment. And having a highly competitive nature, I was challenged to achieve weekly and monthly goals. I was enthusiastic and discovered a spring in my step I had long ago lost.

In making new side-gig friends, I heard their stories and learned the reasons they were working a side-gig. Their "Why's" were genuine and often deeply profound; perhaps it was to be able to put new shoes on their child's feet, pay large unexpected medical bills or their mortgage because they had lost their job, get themselves out of an abusive relationship, have spending flexibility, or maybe it wasn't about the money at all, but rather a place to find camaraderie amongst likeminded people.

I found a unique group of people who are limitless as they dream about their future; who set goals and go after them; and believe they are worthy of having whatever their heart's desire. They know they can improve their lives and the future of their families and community through their side-gig. These people became my friends. They encouraged me, cheered me on and helped me to believe that the opportunity in front of me was only limited by the belief I had in myself. I was discovering that I was worthy of all the goodness life has to offer. WOW!

I wanted to be successful in my side-gig, so I was coachable; I utilized every tool available to me and I attended meetings and trainings. I reached out to others and cheered them on in the fashion I had enjoyed, and most importantly, I dove deeply into personal development to improve my mindset. I began dreaming of a life where I was my own boss, of having time freedom and of helping others remember how to dream and to coach them on how they could reach and fulfill their dreams, too.

My New Life as an MLM Entrepreneur

While I had enjoyed my career, it was a means to an end. It provided me with a wonderful lifestyle, but I was never deeply passionate about it. I envied those who had found their passion, who bounded out of bed in the morning and looked forward to going to work each day and got their energy and zest for life from their work. I never thought I would find that, until I found Network Marketing! Here, I had found my passion! Where corporate life was often filled with toxic environments, high stress and pressure, my side-gig was positive, uplifting, fun and energizing! It was an amazing addition to my life.

I was able to easily integrate my side-gig into my crazy corporate life and found success rather quickly by hitting short-term goals and even being one of the first in my new company to earn the 5-star, all inclusive, incentive trip for two to Cancun (I have gifted the trips to my sister and my best friend. We had a fabulous time making memories without spending a dime!) My side-gig was rewarding me for just doing my "job" and my fellow side-gig colleagues were genuinely happy for me and my success. I was blown away by the overall encouragement and support.

And something interesting happened. As I co-mingled my side-hustle and my corporate job, I became a better employee, a stronger manager and coach to my staff, a more focused friend and happier person overall. My side-hustle was positively impacting every area of my life.

During the recent pandemic, I took a leap of faith and decided to implement my Exit Strategy much sooner than expected. I left my corporate life behind to fully embrace my entrepreneurial-self and made my side-gig my "full-time-gig." I believed that if I worked half as hard for myself as I had for the companies I'd worked for, I'd be more than fine. I had watched people in my MLM rise in rank by utilizing the same products and tools that I had been accessing and I thought "Why can't that be me?" After all, the beauty of Network Marketing is that it is a uniquely level playing field where anyone, regardless of age, gender, education, experience, or socio-economic status can jump in at any time. In Network Marketing, the opportunity for success and unlimited growth is available to all who are willing to work for it.

Being my own boss has been an incredible gift that I gave to myself. I enjoy time freedom and making my own schedule; I can spend quality time, especially during the week with friends; I am available to attend events and am able to be there when people need me, whether near or far.

However, being my own boss did come with some challenges. Procrastination was my arch enemy. Self-imposed deadlines were considered flexible and often missed because after all, the only one being affected was me. I squandered my time because now, I had lots of time, today, tomorrow, next week. In the past, I had a sense of financial security and had been accustomed to getting a regular paycheck that I could relax and depend upon. In Network Marketing, you get out of it what you put into it. Like everything, success requires dedicated time, attention, and commitment. Unfortunately, I let the procrastination get the better of me and it was reflected in my side-gig paycheck! YIKES! I had to become a better boss of me. Thank goodness for personal development helping me refine my self-management skills.

Network Marketing has enriched my life in ways I could not imagine. It has provided the gift of freedom to choose where I work, how I work and when I work. It has given me the opportunity to travel to fun and exciting locations for business and pleasure; afforded me the means to support my philanthropic interests, drive my dream car (a Limited Victory Edition XK8 convertible Jaguar), and has taught me that I AM in control of my life. I have met incredible people and developed life-long friendships. I've stepped out of my comfort zone and have learned to appreciate that only by trying something new amid fear do I grow;

that personal development is a daily necessity, and that my dreams are only limited by my belief that I am worthy.

Just A little Advice

Be Coachable

Do yourself a favor and learn from those who are successful. Successful Network Marketers have ridden the rollercoaster and know how to accelerate the highs and navigate the lows. Your upline knows how to support you and will be there to cheer you on every step of the way!

Invest in Personal Development

The greatest investment you can make is in yourself. Personal development isn't just for those in Network Marketing but should be a part of everyone's life journey. Investing in personal development will help you be your best you.

Do it Afraid

Be willing to step outside your comfort zone and try something new. Enjoy the exhilaration of knowing, YOU DID IT!

Have Fun

Enthusiasm is contagious and will get you everywhere.

Believe in Yourself

Know that you are worthy of everything your heart desires and then GO FOR IT!

Karen is a success-driven, self-motivated professional with a proven track record of accomplishments and leadership-skills. Since discovering Network Marketing, Karen has become an advocate for the industry. Her experience as a successful Network Marketer has taught her that "You will have whatever you believe."

With a Master of Public Administration, Karen has an eclectic background that includes, holding top-secret clearances as a U.S. Federal Government Investigator, traveling the world working in the Entertainment Department onboard luxury cruise ships, and as a corporate Road Warrior supporting educational institutions, among other worthy positions. Adding to her credits, she had an article published in the Autumn 1989 edition of the *Public Budgeting and Finance Journal* including an interview with former CIA Director, Leon Panetta.

Karen is an enthusiastic life-learner and is willing to try nearly anything new. As an adult, she began tap, jazz and ballet dancing, performed in local dance showcases, pre-professional ballets, cabarets and musicals, and she can be seen as an "Extra" in an award-winning independent movie. She enjoys meeting people and making new friends, traveling, golfing, classic movies from the 30's and 40's, and silent film.

Karen lives in Tampa, Florida.

Enthusiasm is contagious and will get you everywhere.

SHARON MEFFORD

"It is what it is. Harvest the good, forgive the rest and move on." Bob Proctor

SHARON MEFFORD

Becoming the person I am meant to be

Growing up, my family and I moved every two or three years. Military life is like that. While it was exciting to live in so many places, it didn't seem like I belonged anywhere. I am child number five out of eight, and I had a heart defect that was diagnosed when I was a toddler. At first my parents were told to keep me from any activity, but keeping a toddler inactive was difficult. Since my Mom didn't work outside the home, even though she was a registered nurse, she watched me like a hawk. She became aware that when I was active, my heart wasn't murmuring like it was when I was inactive, and that surprised her. She then decided to let me be a child and run with my friends and siblings.

Almost every summer, we would visit my Dad's Mom. She would spoil us by taking us shopping and bringing little farm animals over; "Giving the city children a taste of the country", I think is how she put it. I remember her having a beautiful garden and I loved helping her harvest. I was ignorant about what it took to grow beautiful vegetables like she did, but I saw how much love and hard work she put into her garden. I knew that someday I would have a beautiful garden, too.

As my family and I continued to move to different places, it seemed harder for me to make friends. Most children I met had lived in their neighborhoods since birth. So, I was more apt to stay home and help my grandmother and Mom cook and bake. I enjoyed cooking delicious meals, baking cookies, pastries and making all sorts of candy, but most of all I enjoyed being with them because they accepted me. This pattern of behavior, though comfortable at the time, contributed to my isolation and lack of friends. Looking back, I can see where my shyness and unhealthy eating habits came from.

Sports became my passion in high school, providing me with an easy way to fit in. I found that I was quickly accepted onto sports teams when we moved to new places. Though I loved playing sports, I kept many of my insecurities hidden and was very critical of my talent and ability, not believing my coaches who kept me on their teams. Only my two closest friends knew how I felt. Since both of them were very similar to me, it remained a secret.

I noticed an internal shift though, while attending college. At the time, all students were required to spend their first year living in a dorm on campus, even if they lived in town. The first few months were rough for so many students who had to leave home for the first time. I discovered that spending my childhood moving around so much had actually set me up with an advantage. I knew how to handle this kind of change, and my courage and self-confidence soared.

My roommate was from Micronesia, an island nation east of the Philippines, and had lived a sheltered life. She was homesick and during school breaks, she came home with me. It was fun to have someone that was in awe of everything from snow to electric blankets and indoor washers and dryers. It was during that first year that I knew I wanted to be a teacher. As an educator I could help students who were struggling, so physical education and coaching became my goal. A few years later, getting a Special Education Endorsement gave me my first teaching job.

Teaching was the profession that began my transformation from insecure to confident in my ability to affect positive changes in others. As I worked with my students, who weren't expected to go to college, and hopefully get them enough training to have a basic job, I realized that I was beginning to change, gaining confidence as they gained skills. While coaching sports kept me active, the students in my classes were teaching me that everyone has a calling and I was going to help them find their calling. As I continued teaching, the job became very stressful and time consuming. It became more about paperwork and bureaucracy and less and less about teaching. I was working 12-hour days! As a result of that, when I let go of the stress and relaxed on school breaks, I would get very ill. Thanksgiving, Christmas, Spring Break, and right after school let out for the summer. It was like clockwork, and I started to dread breaks.

So, in 2004, when my beautician introduced me to my current network marketing business and the health and wellness products I am still taking and selling now, I thought it was a gift. Healthy eating just got easier. I was able to add vegetables that I didn't like to my regular diet with the capsules. My mom at this time was in the final stages of Alzheimer's. My grandmother had passed away while I was in college, complications from obesity and diabetes. It was then I realized that their health and wellness was directly connected to their food and nutrition choices. Since education was second nature to me, I read up on the products and looked at the research. I purchased it for myself and my husband, but gave them to my parents when he refused to take them. It wasn't a cure, but it gave my dad energy and my mom better health during that last year and I am forever grateful for that time.

My business remained a hobby for a long time because, growing up, I was led to believe that working long hours at a job was the only acceptable form of employment. It was only later on, after working with my mentor and mindset coach, that I realized I was *surrounded* by successful entrepreneurs, even within my own company.

My husband began to take the products in 2006 on a friend's recommendation. Remember, I had been trying to get him to take them for a couple of years at that point. He joined me in the business for a few years because his friend joined the business. Even though he wasn't passionate about building his business, he had amazing success with introducing these fabulous products to many people and helping change many lives. He enjoyed traveling to various places for company gatherings and meeting and talking to people. He considered himself successful, but he did not see himself as an entrepreneur. I am grateful that he continues to take the products and share their benefits. I believe he is an entrepreneur at heart.

Remembering how I loved my grandmother's garden? I planted one at our first house. Well, I wasn't prepared for the bugs, slugs and squirrels competing for my produce. It was a disaster and I didn't garden again until 2013 when I purchased an indoor/outdoor vertical garden. This is an amazing system for growing year-round indoors or outdoors. I currently own two of them and enjoy planting celery, yellow squash, cucumbers, peppers, herbs, spinach, kale, all sorts of lettuces, and rooting other plants to give away as gifts. Recently, I accepted the challenge to grow watermelons. I don't know if it will work, but I am willing to give it a go because watermelons are delicious and I love challenges!

In 2015, I experienced burnout. The long hours and "never enough time to get everything done" led me to take early retirement. I was not passionate about going to work and it affected my mental health. The students I worked with picked up on the change, and I knew it was time to leave. I then began the process of turning my part-time teaching healthy eating and living hobby into a true full-time entrepreneurial business. I was becoming a leader and empowering other women to add to their income. We went to events, put on events and were enjoying life. I was making the life of my dreams. Life was amazing.

In 2018, I had total knee replacement surgery. Somewhere in the recovery process, I began doubting my skills and things began falling apart. I had been told in elementary school: "Sharon, you are smart, go back to your desk and figure it out". After receiving this message repeatedly, asking for help wasn't easy. However, I knew I needed help to get my excitement back and I set out to find help.

I paid counselors, went to seminars, read self-help books, attended many network-marketing events, and the list goes on. Nothing seemed to be changing except I was losing hope and a lot of money. I was on one of my company's weekly calls and heard a woman speak about mindset and the importance of getting it aligned with your goal. I was intrigued. She was scheduled to be a speaker at the bootcamp I was attending the next weekend. She offered to meet me there for a conversation, because to me, it was too good to be true. We met and as I visited with her, I realized that she believed in mentoring as part of the program, not just a couple times, but for a year minimum. I joined her program the Monday I returned from bootcamp. As I became immersed in the program, I was challenged to change my beliefs about myself that I had since childhood and to get out of my comfort zone. All of this was done with what I call tough love because I resisted at times while my mentor kept believing in me and challenged me to make small changes.

During one session when she asked me about forgiveness, I said, "Sure I forgive people, I do it all the time". She asked me about a couple of examples and I told her how they had wronged me. She replied that I hadn't really forgiven them. So, I did the work, but something was still nagging me and I would get upset when she asked me about them. Like the wise person she is, she asked, "have you forgiven yourself?" I said, "What's to forgive? I haven't wronged myself". We had a fairly long discussion on forgiveness. I was still under the belief that saying I was sorry was sufficient. I also believed that letting go of the hurt or anger meant to forget it and I was not going to let that person hurt me again. I finally began to understand what true forgiveness really meant. It freed me up from the self-torment and I got the "real-estate" back in my mind for better thoughts. It was the best thing that ever happened to me! It was life changing! I let go of past hurts. I let go of many beliefs I had held onto because they came from family members I respected. These were beliefs that no longer served me and were holding me back, like "being an entrepreneur isn't a real job".

As I forgave myself, I realized that in many instances, a little girl was controlling my decision making. Self-limiting beliefs I had held transformed:

"You are a smart girl, go back and figure it out" became *"Together we Thrive"*

"You don't deserve happiness" became *"You deserve all the happiness in the world, so do what makes you happy"*

I still find beliefs that no longer serve me, but I am releasing them and forgiving myself for holding on to them for so long. With my new abundance mindset, I began seeing others as teammates instead of competition. Having friends in my business and in different network marketing companies is such an amazing way to build relationships, customers and Team. The thrill of being with people who are in various network marketing companies opens the door to more possibilities. I am inspired daily to serve others better because I am surrounded with like-minded individuals who choose to be open to working together to bring health, abundance and happiness to everyone they meet.

I was challenged by my mentor to get into online networking groups and actually worked as a franchisee for a year with a company that had zoom meetings for buying and selling products and services. Joining the various group meetings and getting in front of others tested my self-image, but the rewards and the confidence that it built, and continues to build, have been amazing.

Remember the shy girl from the early days? She is cheering me on instead of holding me back.

As I look back on this journey, I realize that I had to go through everything I did in order to become the person I am today. While the journey isn't even close to being over, reflecting on my decision to stay in the business leads me to a few observations.

OBSERVATIONS

One: The happiness I experience when people tell me stories of how the products I sell have improved their lives and the lives of their children and friends.

Two: The joy I experience hearing gardening stories and seeing people blossom when they share successes, challenges, and the laughter that accompanies the stories. Many people do not believe they have the talent or a "green thumb" for gardening, and when they are successful, it surprises them and they absolutely light up. It's such a buzz!

Three: The thrill of watching shifts in mindset and witnessing how people change when they believe in themselves and become their own best friend. This affects all areas of their life and those around them. I know this first hand, and when I see others' confidence blossom, it inspires me to keep doing what I'm doing.

Four: The commitment I have made to myself to encourage healthy living in body, mind and Spirit is why I stay. I have not found a better way to get and stay healthy.

Five: With incredible friendships and inspiration, the team of people that surrounds me consistently feeds me what I need in order to continue making changes that impact others in positive, life-changing ways. Writing this chapter opened up my life even more. I've met and continue to learn from the authors in this book. I am grateful for the experience and encourage everyone to get out of their comfort zone and write. It's an amazing way to grow yourself and your business.

Six: The best is yet to come. Each day is a new page in my book of life. I have a routine to assist me in making sure every day starts out amazing. I keep it going knowing that I have support from my growing group of friends. There are people to meet, lives to change, and lessons to learn. I am embracing each day and learning to stay present in each activity. It is such a rewarding time to be in network marketing.

Seven: There is no ceiling to how much I can earn as an entrepreneur. As a teacher, there was a maximum. I now realize that I am able to earn as much money as I want, there is no limit.

BIGGEST LESSON

My biggest lesson was to stop following people who tried things for a short period and were always searching for faster ways to make more money in the business. I was doing that and spent thousands of dollars and hours being critical of myself for not keeping up on what I termed, "the flavor of the month". I began to see that being consistent and persistent in approach is crucial, and repetition is what really works for me.

Once I realized I needed the repetition, I went back to the notes I took, and the books I read once and put on the shelf. I began reading and rereading, contacting some of the people whose names I had written in the margins and asking questions, internalizing parts that spoke to me. So much more of my world opened up to me, I was amazed. It was me being true to myself and the power that followed was incredible! Instead of the "flavor of the month", *"harvesting the good, forgiving the rest and moving on"* became my mantra.

ADVICE

The one piece of advice I would share is to get quiet and listen to your inner voice. It takes practice, but when you do, amazing things happen. I am doing things that a year or two ago I would not have attempted because I now get quiet every morning and ask, "What's the plan for today, for my businesses and me personally"?

Sharon was a school teacher and sports coach for 27 years. Now she is an Author, Entrepreneur and a Success Advisor enjoying the freedom and abundance of being her own boss, as well as traveling and making friends around the world. She is grateful for the opportunities and growth that both her health and wellness business and her mindset coaching business provide her as she continues her focus on healthy longevity for everyone she meets.

Harvest the good,

forgive the rest,

and move on.

MELANIE BOOHER

"Good people will come for your mission/values, but they will stay based on how they are treated."

MELANIE BOOHER

Thoughts from A Unicorn Salesperson

"You know, you really are a unicorn, right?" This was recently said to me by a trusted and admired colleague. In fact, just restating it makes me smile! Her compliment was to reference the fact that she believes I'm a unique rarity - one who is good at my career, but who also has a knack for selling. This combo is not a normal feat! The best part is, I really don't think about it as sales at all ... just building relationships and helping people solve their business problems related to people.

Growing up as an athlete and being really competitive, does it surprise you that I also wanted to be one of the top-sellers of Girl Scout cookies? Then, after college, I started a business selling jewelry with my friend. I loved finding a need and filling the gap. As I became a mom and organizing my home became more important, I started selling a Network Marketing company based around organizing. If you walk through my house today, you'll find tons of those products in just about every room in the house! What I liked most about my new business was hosting parties at houses, creating fun events like girl's nights, and having very natural conversations about my products. Hosting a party, having a few beverages and appetizers, while chatting with other ladies about some of your favorite topics made selling fun and easy. Again, easily filling a need through conversations and building relationships.

I sold naturally with my people-driven, relationship-building style. I was able to build a team and advance. It was a fun and worthwhile side business, something that I did alongside my main gig. In retrospect, building my home party business helped me learn many of the details necessary to run my other business. Whether it was tracking expenses, reaching out to new people, building relationships, the importance of networking, creating the foundation that a solid business is built upon, learning to appreciate the word "No", and finding ideas to overcome it or know when to walk away. It was during this time that I learned that the word "No" often really just means, "not right now". That understanding helped me build resilience and the tenacity needed to stay the course. Because of all this, I credit my Network Marketing business as the launching pad that gave me the confidence needed to continue with my main business. Aside from the information that I learned from both my Network Marketing business and my main business, I also loved the idea and practice of gig-economy fractional sales!

During the time of the pandemic, I made many changes so that I could sustain and grow my businesses, and as well, I did some very important personal development. I made some critical decisions to improve my ability to take on more work, to grow and to scale.

It was during this time my trusted colleague made the comment about my skills as a unicorn. I'm an expert in my field with strong networks, great relationships, and am fabulous at creating opportunities. I embraced my sales skills with new thoughts: "I'm a unicorn, I love my trade, believe greatly in my work, and am making the world better".

Additionally, I challenged my internal narrative related to selling. I had gone my whole life demonizing sales as this elusive and difficult thing. I would stress over my belief that sales was too much outside my comfort zone, too numbers driven, too high-achievement based, and too scary to handle without a sales certification or formal education.

STOP. I had become my own worst enemy and allowed this perception of sales to be a bully in our relationship! I took an intentional moment to regroup, analyze, and rephrase all of this. I challenged old notions that had taken over healthy thoughts related to sales.

Selling *is* within my comfort zone. In fact, I have discovered over the years that I actually enjoy (dare I say LOVE) sales! Not only did I like it, I'm actually pretty darn good at it. Numbers proved it. Others saw more sales ability in me than I saw in myself, and they continually built up my confidence. I realized that I did not need a special certification or formal education, I had 20+ years of business experience and 15 years of relationship selling as I ran my own businesses. I had strong sense of self and resilience to push forward, even when others might deter my efforts (e.g. saying no!), and a lifetime of watching, learning, and experiencing human nature.

Like any good unicorn - I have to stop and think about what makes my style uniquely stand out from the rest. I think many of the top leaders that I associate with have stories like mine, they just haven't taken the time to assess their success factors.

So, what core components do I attribute to my Network Marketing experience aiding in my business success to this point in my career and helping me become a sales unicorn?

- ***Business Acumen***: It created the foundation of support and administrative know-how that I needed to build a well-running business.
- ***Relationship Focus***: It focused my attention on relationships, both related to tapping into my network for ongoing support and growth, and the kind of people with whom I'd want to build a business.
- ***Owner-Minded***: It reminded me why I wanted to run my own business in the first place: for increased schedule flexibility and balance with my family life

- ***Performance Driven***: It gave me the drive to sell and beat sales numbers / perform at a higher level as I built my own team and competed for prizes, awards and/or accolades.

- ***Entrepreneurial Passion***: It fostered the pride that I have as an entrepreneur and business owner, being seen as a leader who gets stuff done and isn't afraid to try something new.

- ***Growth-Minded***: It reminded me of the need for continuing education and the importance of being a life-long learner (that's why those team meetings, national support, mentoring relationships, and annual conferences are so amazing!)

- ***Resilience***: It gave me plenty of opportunities to deal with difficult people, to hear the word "No" and keep moving forward without getting feelings hurt.

- ***Social Element***: It instilled a healthy appreciation for the social side of business. Whether networking, girl's nights, happy hours, home parties - having fun with others is key to enjoying your work!

- ***Presentation Skills***: It afforded me the opportunity to hone my skills in presenting in front of others (over and over again!) so that I could perfect my pitch and overcome public speaking fears.

- ***Confidence***: It allows entrepreneurs to dig into their business at their own pace, growing one referral / sale at a time, understanding more and more with every sale, and building the confidence to lead yourself and others.

- ***Shared Experience***: It's a path that you never have to travel by yourself, fostering support and mentoring from all sides and opening doors for others to be part of something great with you!

Sharing these components for success, learned from Network Marketing and applied throughout my business journey, brings me great joy. I've made it my mission to share freely and extend my hands to guide others. I extend my hands to those courageous leaders trying to make a difference. I extend my hands to those leaders trying to shift the tides or change the narrative, trying to get rid of bad habits and instill positive ones. I extend my hands to make small, intentional changes. To make them *great*, and to be the change we want to see in the world.

Given all of this, I've come to the realization that being a sales unicorn isn't really magic at all. It's a series of making good choices, learning from key past experiences, building into others, valuing others and their experience, knowledge, and network, leading with heart, and extending your hands over and over to raise others up.

This book is an example of how we share. We extend our hands to those a few steps behind. Come with us on this unique journey, our hands are extended to you.

Melanie Booher is a Culture Coach & Personal Brand Coach, trainer, speaker, international #1 best selling author, owns a media and publication company, and is the creator of Cards for Culture©

She has a Bachelor's Degree from Miami University and a Master's in HR from the University of Cincinnati.

Melanie lives outside of Cincinnati, Ohio with her husband (Matt), 3 children (McKenna, Madilynn, and Matheson) and 2 fur babies (Grady and Pepper).

DANIKA ADAMTHWAITE

"When you have nothing to work against, you have everything to work towards."

DANIKA ADAMTHWAITE

I remember putting shapes into a ball. When all the shapes were in the ball, you could pull it open, dump the shapes out, and start again. Our doctor's office had a set of blocks that opened up on a diagonal, and you could snap them to other blocks in a long chain like a snake. I loved those blocks.

I remember friends whose mothers had boxes of stuff they sold from home. My mom took me to parties with her, and I remember her dislike for hosting them because no one showed up. We had a huge plastic bowl that we mostly used for popcorn growing up. I say 'mostly' because it worked overtime as the "puke" bowl in our house, a constant companion when my sister and I were sick. Sharing that as an adult, I am always surprised to hear how many people grew up with one of these bowls and played with those toys. It wasn't until I had kids of my own that I connected to where those toys came from, and I still use one of those bowls for my kids. And popcorn.

When I became interested in makeup as a teenager, my mom took me to a lady for a lesson in makeup and skincare. As I'm thinking back and remembering little snippets of my past, I see how network marketing companies were in my life long before I even knew what that was. That didn't mean anything to me growing up, and it would be years before I learned anything about network marketing.

I was in my early twenties when I met Crystal at a makeup party. I liked that she was vibrant and confident. I didn't wear makeup often but felt compelled to say yes when she presented the business opportunity to me that night. I did nothing with that business, but I will never forget how Crystal made me feel. She saw something in me that I didn't. I said yes to Crystal, not the product or the company, but the woman standing in front of me. In the end, our connection went beyond business and remained a lifelong friendship.

Within weeks of meeting Crystal, I reconnected with my best friend from junior high, Mike. He was living in Vancouver and working as an Actor. We hadn't seen each other or spoken in well over a year. After a few weeks of phone calls, he flew me down from Prince George to celebrate my birthday. On my first day, there was a whirlwind of activity; breakfast out, a hike in the woods, shopping, lunch, a cafe with a four-string quartet, followed by dinner and dancing. It was a magical day, and I didn't want it to end. The following day we were exhausted. Mike still had to work while I slept in and had a lazy morning. We had no plans other than to enjoy each other's company.

After enduring such a long separation over the years, I opened up to him. I didn't want only to see him once every couple of years, and I wanted more; he did too! So, we settled on that. We wanted to be together. It was a few more hours before I asked how we were physically going to do this. I had a townhouse in another city to deal with, two jobs to go back to, and the planner in me was getting anxious.

Without hesitation, Mike asked, "Well, do you want to marry me?"

I said yes.

By the end of the first year of our engagement, we'd learned a lot about each other, ourselves, and what we wanted. We talked about my desire to travel, and we agreed there was no rush for a wedding just yet. I had only left the country once when I was 12, but that trip to Hawaii rooted itself deeply in my soul, and travel became a deep passion for me. I still travel whenever I get the chance.

After high school and before reuniting with Mike, my love for travel led me to enroll in a Travel Agent Program in my childhood hometown of Victoria. I found everything about it fascinating and was eager to start. I had barely finished my program when I was needed back home in Prince George to help my parents with their custom furniture business. I felt like I was going backward, but I had finished school with no real plan, and travel agents can work anywhere, right?

Eventually, my mother wanted me to join her on a product buying trip to Vancouver. I jumped at the chance. Unfortunately, our trip was cut short by 9/11, and we returned home right away. I never did work in tourism after that, but knowledge gained is never lost.

Once Mike and I settled into our new sense of togetherness, we agreed that I would take work abroad to feed that travel hunger and still make some money. I went to Italy to be an Au Pair. It was a disastrous situation that I quickly and wisely exited. It was evident that my employment opportunity was not at all what I had hoped it would be. I put the experience behind me and chose to take advantage of the circumstances as they were. I travelled all over Italy and fed that hunger. Two weeks later, my spirit full of the beauty of Italy, I flew back home to my future husband. In the following year, we were busy buying our first house, welcoming our first baby, AND getting married.

When our second baby came, I knew I wouldn't be returning to work outside of the home. Network Marketing would allow me to stay home and bring in grocery money. I was open to learning about the companies behind the products I liked and already used, many of which came from these companies we all grew up with. Despite enjoying some products, I wasn't finding the right fit.

I was learning and searching for something, and I simply didn't know what yet. As Mike and I searched, we took a chance on an opportunity with a newer network marketing company, and we decided to work it together. We worked hard selling and sharing, selling and sharing. We did the calls, training, private training dinners with the Executive Team, and conferences. We did well in a short amount of time, but we were stressed out.

Consumed by deadlines and training that promised more of the same, I couldn't rid myself of this nagging feeling that something wasn't quite right. When rumours started to surface about the company and CEO, it was enough for us to trust our gut and walk away. The company was bought out within a year, and the CEO was gone. We felt like failures, and we wouldn't feel anything like that again. It was a huge lesson in what we didn't want and trusting ourselves when something didn't feel right.

I keep coming back to Network Marketing for my family. Not just for the range of products I've discovered that answer my family's varied needs. The education and continued knowledge that I have gleaned from my experiences alone benefit my family. Network Marketing is responsible for many of the lessons I can share with the future adults I am raising. I've learned to create balance in my life and strive to teach them to do the same in the smaller scope of their day or week. I want them to make conscious choices with kindness and care about helping people. My children instinctively raise those around them. The lessons of positivity and team building abound in our house since I have four children. I want them to know how to balance the care of others with care for themselves. I want them to trust their intuition and seek guidance when they need it. I want to be able to support them however I can, and the more knowledge I have, the more I can pass on to them.

These businesses and opportunities have brought some amazing women into my life. I'm grateful for their friendships and support. The businesses themselves taught me about my health and personal growth. I couldn't find one that fit me despite trying, again and again, only to be able to cherry-pick the things I did like from each company's lessons. The community of support. The friendships and contacts I made. The opportunities to see places I may not have travelled to on my own. The biggest challenge I discovered was that I am my biggest challenge.

I overcommit. I have a hard time saying no to people--just like I couldn't say no to Crystal all those years ago. I was distracted and wanted to be able to do everything and help everyone. I couldn't understand how all these women I had met had this boundless enthusiasm. How did they harness all this time and energy and get so much done? I was only genuinely successful if I let things get to a point where it was now or never and do or die trying. I tried setting goals and creating timelines but constantly got distracted by some other task that was now in that 'now or never' window. I would convince myself things were more important, and this constant argument in my brain was wasting my mental energy. I was a mess.

It wasn't until a couple of years ago when my second child was diagnosed with ADHD, that I started connecting some dots. While trying to educate myself on how best to help my child through something I didn't know much about, I fell into a rabbit hole. The more I read, the more I began to identify my struggles in my youth. Nearly everything was like turning on a spotlight on my life. I could think back to my school days and all my struggling attempts to get a business off the ground and see where my ADHD helped and hindered me in my journey. I began to understand, not just my child's struggles, but also myself. I can pass on all I have learned to them, and I feel the same about everything I learned in Network Marketing. I can apply my knowledge to my life every day--who would have known the team I was managing would be quite so rambunctious?

I've learned to choose wisely. When to hold and build up energy and when to release that energy and grow. I tried to do it all in my early years and burned myself out. Physically, emotionally and mentally, I was drained. I had health issues, and so did others in my family. I had two kids in school and two more little ones at home. I was all over the place, overextending myself as a volunteer, going back to school, and trying to start a business simultaneously. Looking back now, I see why I struggled to find that balance. To find something means you lost something, but I had not lost my balance. I never really had that balance. I had to learn to create that balance in my life, and to do that, I'd have to take care of myself.

On airplanes, they tell you to put your mask on first before assisting others? That's good advice. If my mental health wasn't being cared for, how could I expect my children to be able to care for their own? Network Marketing taught me to lead by example--so I did.

Everyone talks about finding your 'Why'. Why do you want to do this? What do you want to accomplish? What is your reason for doing this? Employers ask, 'Why do you want this job?' The obvious answer is because I want money so I can live. I always assumed there was some correct answer people were looking for. I did workshops, worked with coaches and companies, and tried to figure out what they wanted to hear. Answering this question almost paralyzed me mentally.

I know it's not the money. It's the travel. It's my kids. It's putting dinner on the table and showing them the world. It's the knowledge and learning I have gained. The friends I made. The people I met and the places I went. I can take everything I've learned in my successes and failures and pass that knowledge on to the adults I'm raising right now.

I spent years discovering that the something I was searching for each time was knowledge. To learn and grow and share. Kindly and from my heart. I want to choose myself and, to stop working against myself. There are enough people out there who don't want to see others succeed that I don't need to stand in my own way.

The journey has not been comfortable, but growth seldom is. Change is uncomfortable, but it is also liberating. Growing up, we were told that you could do whatever you can put your mind to, but what if your mind was a basket of cats?

I could see the goals I was striving toward, but putting the steps together to reach that goal was like herding kittens back into a box. Network Marketing taught me how to break these monumental tasks into smaller achievable steps, and the skills I gained helped my business grow and change to become precisely what I need it to be. I couldn't be more grateful to be in an industry that offers the flexibility that I need daily to allow my family to thrive.

Like so many times before, I doubted that I could write this. I didn't know where to begin or what to say. Did I have anything worth saying? Worth reading? I almost said no. That would have been a mistake. This experience has been scary and enlightening, and I would have regretted saying no. Writing this has been daunting. I leaned heavily on what I've learned in Network Marketing, by breaking it down into achievable steps, executing them promptly, and trusting the advice of my team.

I said yes because I knew I would learn something from it. I didn't know what that would be and didn't need to. Nothing changes by saying no. Say yes more often when opportunity knocks, and you'll never stop learning. Every lesson is one more brick in the foundation of your success. Each brick builds you up into a more successful version of yourself. Remove yourself as an obstacle to your success.

When you have nothing to work against, you have everything to work towards.

DEBORAH DRUMMOND

"Faith is a significant component of Success."

DEBORAH DRUMMOND

I'm eight years old at the front door, and I'm excited. I am watching my mom pack her products that we're going to set up in my aunt's living room. I get to go work with my mom. She was a home party representative. I loved the feeling of hanging out with the ladies. I felt grown-up, and I enjoyed watching the women having fun, shopping, and laughing.

That was my first introduction to Network Marketing, it created great memories. In my late teens, my mother got involved in a clothing company, and you know what? I had the same happy experience, my girlfriends getting together, laughing, having fun, and my mother selling out of her products night after night. It was a win-win and everyone had a good time. It really impressed upon me a feeling of community and commerce. The women there really enjoyed shopping with my mom. It made them happy knowing they were buying products they were excited to get and you could feel how good they felt knowing they were supporting their friend. So, I have to say, that's probably part of the reason that when I got the vision to start my own home party company, I went for it.

Now to paint the scenario, I was a single mom of a beautiful young daughter, starting my own business for the first time. This was over 25 years ago; women entrepreneurs were not typical. Nor was the decision to launch two companies at once, both in health and wellness. Aromatherapy and gemstone jewelry were still unknown.

The story of how I created two home party companies for 17 years is an incredible journey meant to be its own book one day. My love for

Network Marketing when I went into those companies was the same when I came out. I have never doubted the power of this system. To be able to have your own business, with everything done for you, that you can do on your time, and around your own life said two things to me, and I believed for everyone: Freedom and Relief. Throughout the time I owned my home party companies, I had also kept my traditional business of a holistic wellness spa going as well. Life was full, but I loved helping people and so did my incredible staff.

When I got invited back into Network Marketing, I simply agreed to help a fellow entrepreneur by letting her share her product with me. When she asked me to look at the business, I nicely said *no*. She didn't know everything that was going on in my life. I was going through a marital status change, becoming a single mom of two children, had 18 staff, my business was open seven days a week, and we were booked 12 hours a day, three weeks ahead.

When she was telling me the company story, my head was saying *no*, but my gut was screaming *yes*. I said I was too busy, and she said, *"I will back you all the way."* Those were powerful words for me. Her words felt like relief. She was smart enough to give me a sample. I came home, gave it to my daughter, and she had amazing results; we both joined the company, and the rest is history.

I wasn't lying when I said I had no time. I sacrificed little things, I had to really structure the power of my moments, and I'd text every moment I had free. That's why I love Network Marketing; it's a group effort. When I was up against the clock, I could call people to help, which is very different from traditional business.

I've chosen this as a career, the products and the company I am with, because it has allowed me to offer an extension of what I believe in, which is Preventative Health and Entrepreneurial Wealth. Being the traditional business owner that I was, I always thought about legacy. I knew I was creating this business for myself, but I also built it for my family's financial future. Being a single mom, I knew that sometimes it's all on you, and you need to find the courage to go *all in*.

There have been wins and accomplishments I have been able to experience in my Network Marketing business—most of them, a complete surprise. I didn't expect the awards and perks, international travel, recognition from my peers, lifelong friendships and a plethora of incredible industry people that are living a fulfilled life.

Above all of the perks I have received, spending time in this industry, working and building with my daughter is incredible. As a result of being raised in an entrepreneurial-minded home, my son decided to be an entrepreneur at age 15 and started his own company. This makes me grateful to this industry. If you are a parent or a grandparent, (and I'm both), I can tell you first hand it's been a sheer blessing to have entrepreneurship as part of our family's life. It has shown my children that life is what you make it. It has taught my children that there is always a way, a solution to any problem that arises in our home. If we needed something for our health, education, home, bills, school fees, or whatever, we had a vehicle to do something about it. We at least had a choice to take this opportunity we had in front of us and put in some extra effort, if we needed something quickly or if we had an emergency.

I have been able to be a career mom and a mom that can take the day off from work to go to the school concerts, special events or vacation when we wanted; based on our dates not someone else's. I got to be in the best of both worlds and I am grateful.

It was such a proactive way to raise my children. They saw responsibility in a different way. It has allowed them to choose their life paths knowing the options that entrepreneurship can offer.

We now have a new generation in our family and this "Freedom YaYa" is pretty excited about that!

People have told me that they see me as driven, but I would correct it by saying that I'm FILLED WITH PURPOSE. The word 'driven' has been given a bad rap. So many people I see are fuelled by their own passions and, although it looks like they're driven, they are really just living their best life! That is a huge part of why I do what I do, and want to share what I have learned with others.

Network Marketing for so many people is a financial purpose-filled vehicle to fuel their dreams and aspirations in other areas. That is what's so exciting!

When I really believe in something, I'm an "*all-in*" woman. Life's not been easy every day just because I made an incredible lifestyle business decision, but with my willingness to learn, my commitment, excitement and desire for a better life for myself and for others, that has been the elixir I've woken up to every morning.

For some people, it's their coffee. For me, it's my fuel.

I was willing to stay up late, get up early, spend money on books and courses, and go to company conferences because they told me it was the best place to move my business quicker. One could even argue that I take as many courses, read more books, hire different coaches as much now as I did at the beginning of my business.

It wasn't funny then, but it's funny now when people tell me, "You deliver presentations so well." They don't remember seeing me at the very beginning of my career when I barely got through a presentation without being full of nerves. I thought I would not make it to the end; all I could do was stand there and say what I knew. I actually used to watch my sponsor do presentations over and over. I would go every week and take written notes. Then, when it was my turn to speak, I would read off of recipe cards. We all have to learn somehow and someway. Do what you have to do to feel confident and don't worry about how good or not perfect it is. This is the beginning cost of a successful business.

My Tell All's That Created My Success

GRACE

The word that comes to me is GRACE. That may not sound like much advice, but it really is. Business isn't always easy. Sometimes we feel confused, we feel we're not getting traction, we get frustrated, and it feels hard. I think *Grace* has brought me out of those places and back into hope and joy.

Grace, for me, gets banked up every time I work my business, do training, have a success, help someone hit a goal, stretch myself, or take a risk. So, when I feel like I'm hitting the wall, all that banked up *Grace* makes tough times easier for me.

PROFESSIONAL HELP

Hiring coaches and professionals who know more than I do in areas I want to improve always was, and still is, the game changer for my success. Never hesitate to seek out help for betterment.

SUCK IT UP AND JUMP

This might sound a little, what some would say, *"Janis Joplin"*, but sometimes YOU JUST GOT TO SUCK IT UP AND JUMP. Sometimes you just got to go *all in,* no matter whether you know if it'll work out or not. Sometimes push comes to shove, and I have to shove myself. I have to take that risk. I have to call that person that I am nervous about, I have to ask for a sale that I might be unsure of, and I have to bypass my own self-defeating talk and tell myself *"no more excuses, no more avoiding, just do it!"*

MUSIC

Here is one more tip that is one of my success secrets on days that I'm not 100 percent feeling "it," I use MUSIC. I find a song that's going to put me in a different headspace, and I listen to it really loud. If I need to feel brave, I listen to *AC/DC*. If I need to get calm and centred, I listen to some *Chris Stapleton*. If I need inspiration, I listen to *Peter Gabriel*. If I want to be kind to myself, I listen to *Loretta Lynn*. If I want to feel safe, I listen to *Fleetwood Mac*. Everyone has their own way of overcoming feelings and thoughts that hold them back. For me, I have found a solution in music. It may sound a little odd or unorthodox, but music has truly made a difference in my business success.

WRITING

Another one of the powerful success tools I will share: WRITE. If you were to look at my desk right now, you would see the writing on whiteboards, paper pads, journals and day timers. I have been called *Paper Girl* more than once. I use a day timer that lines out for me questions that I ask myself in the morning that prompts me to think intentionally about how that day is going to go. I plan the night before my day ahead. I also have a writing system for evaluating my day and how to close my evening out.

MAKING LISTS

Whether it's a grocery list, personal development list, prospect list, Christmas list, goals list, financial goals list, time-lining or self-evaluation, MAKING LISTS has also been a critical part of my business results. These lists are an important part of my strategic plans for my life, my goals, and how I want my business to be in the flow of success and progression.

READING

Lastly, I am an avid reader. READING is crucial to achieving success, in my opinion. As I sit in my home right now, on one chair, there are three books, and there's one book to the left to me, three more books to the right of me and four on my bedside table. I love to read actual books on paper. I love to underline, circle, make a star, and I really like to dog-ear the pages.

For me, this thing called life, of which my career is a part, has been such an untold series of events that I couldn't have put together on my own. I have had to learn to have faith, have patience, and have trust; trust in myself has been one of the biggest lessons in my life. What I do to make this journey better, easier, faster, less painful and more joyful is to do my best to stay aligned with myself and the right people.

I think that this is an incredible industry. I love the magic and hope in it. I've seen people accomplish goals in half the time or double the time, and it can be as frustrating as it is exhilarating. I absolutely love how at the heart of this industry it is about helping others. All we can do is be who we are in what we do, and do the best we can with what we've got. Just know that it will be okay, and you'll be okay.

I have to say sometimes our industry gets a bad rap because people didn't get what they wanted either fast enough, smooth enough or easy enough, or, or, or. There are so many pieces to success in this industry, not unlike traditional business. People leave for whatever reason, and that's okay. I just never want to see anyone go before that tipping point where traction hits the road, and the dreams they so badly wanted for themselves start to come to pass. Don't give up when it gets a little tough, or even a lot! Try to hold on to your vision of what the future has in store for you. In a world that moves at rapid speed, we need to remember it's still one day at a time. Our business is growing one day at a time, we are growing one day at a time. Quitting 100 percent guarantees that your business will not work. Instead, hanging in and figuring out the next step might be tough, but it's only temporarily tough. Sometimes we've got to pull our superhero capes out of the closet and find the miracles. Stick around long enough so you can actually reap the benefits. That's when things really get fun!

I'm thrilled and honoured to be an author in a book whose mandate is to raise the bar on how people see the professionalism of this incredible industry. I genuinely believe that it is an industry for everybody. I've said it before and will always say that, in my opinion, Network

Marketing is the most equal opportunity employer I have yet to see in my lifetime.

Thank you for the opportunity to share. I hope you found something in my story that inspired you, helped you, or even made you laugh.

Network Marketing is the most equal opportunity employer I have yet to see in my lifetime.

GREGORY AND ROBIN BLANC MASCARI

"If it is worth doing, it is worth doing big!"

GREGORY AND ROBIN BLANC MASCARI

We Grow People

Gregory and I have very different backgrounds. We met through an opportunity meeting where he was in the front of the room as a corporate executive and I was a brand-new and excited distributor. It was suggested to me to find a mentor, someone who shared my values. Four years later, Gregory and I were married, the best mentor ever! On my list of what I wanted in a partner was a partner on every level. Little did I know that network marketing was the vehicle that would provide that amazing partnership – bringing out our best – together.

Gregory's background was as an entrepreneur owning a manufacturing business. When he sold his business back in 1988 for the deal that sounded too good to be true and turned out to be so, he needed to find a way to support the family, and network marketing arrived at the right time. After a rough start in the first year having to learn a new profession, he did not give up, and went on to be extraordinarily successful in the field, building several organizations with hundreds of thousands of members. Over the last 33+ years, Gregory has gone from being a successful field leader, a VP of Sales in a well-funded MLM start-up, a company owner, an industry consultant, and finally coming full circle to find his preferred and permanent niche as an independent field leader.

Gregory has always had the philosophy of "If it's worth doing, it's worth doing big!" When I met him back in 2001, I was new to MLM and he certainly expanded my perception of what was possible. His mastery of constantly looking for simpler and simpler ways for the average person to be successful with basic tools has been a huge gift to our teams over the years. Whether it's creating a "Daily Method of Operation" or a "Getting Started Guide," our businesses have thrived because we focus on giving the average person a track to run on, creating a foundation for their success through simplicity and duplication.

After I graduated from the University of Michigan Business School with a degree in marketing, the majority of my pre-MLM career was spent in personal and leadership development in the corporate world, while always being self-employed. We love to say that we are both certifiably unemployable ☺. Working in the outplacement world (career transition), The Covey Leadership Center, Enlightened Leadership, InsideOut Development and other organizations, I was blessed to have many great mentors. My passion for human potential was a driving force in my career and no matter what position I held, each of my career choices involved opportunities for significant personal growth.

I was Blessed to be one of the earliest certified facilitators and licensees for The Covey Leadership Center, and helping to launch the iconic book "Seven Habits of Highly Effective People" by Stephen Covey. From working with Stephen, I learned that it all starts with "private victories preceding public victories." To truly be successful in any profession and in life, we first need to do the personal work. Stephen taught me the invaluable truth of keeping balance in my career, life, home, spirit and relationships, and how important it is that our core values are also satisfied.

When I discovered that network marketing was really a personal development program with a compensation plan, my love of the profession exploded way beyond the products and opportunity. I realized that when properly done, we create something like a human greenhouse -- a safe place for people to grow into their potential.

We've experienced the best and worst of our profession but our love of the business model has never faded. Sadly, many get discouraged when either the company, products or timing don't work out, and they quit. Although we kissed many frogs and have been in a number of companies that did not make it, even when things didn't work out, we did not lose belief in our profession. We brushed ourselves off and kept searching for a place to call home. Both of us were determined, resilient, committed and absolutely knew with the greatest intention that we would create success together, beyond our expectations.

We discovered that when we work together, our success is greatly enhanced. There were several times when we were in different businesses and not only was it not as much fun, our success was also limited.

Our very different gifts, skills and experience along with our aligned values and decisiveness have made our partnership powerful and effective. Our differences create synergy as we complement each other in many areas. We both have a love of helping people grow and creating community in our teams, and the diversity of personalities in our profession can be both exciting and challenging. To this day, when ethical challenges arise, I defer to Gregory's wisdom and experience. I am beyond grateful to know that when a challenging situation surfaces, we will address it in a way that is balanced and objective, making it best for all involved.

Gregory is the strategic planner -- a master at creating tools and systems -- and the organized thinker of our team. I'm more of the relationship-oriented person with a large capacity to love a lot of people and maintain a constant desire to provide opportunities for people's personal and professional growth.

Many years ago in my first networking company, I ended up hosting a weekly personal development call for our team. My love of interviewing turned into a regular program called *30 Minutes of Wisdom,* where I have had the opportunity to interview and share the wisdom of many well-known and not-so-well-known thought leaders. I still do these interviews twice a month, which are a favorite of our team. Although they may not know the speaker, they know they will be provided with valuable insights, resources and tools for their personal and professional development. Along with these programs, we also have incorporated a simple, systematic approach for everyone to be able to coach and grow their people.

Our journey together in network marketing has been quite a roller coaster. We thought that the company we met at was the ONE, but things turned out very differently. We've experienced the best and worst of this profession and are grateful that our love of the profession is stronger than some of the challenging times we have been through. What has created our success is what Gregory calls "failing enough to win"!

We believe that much of our success has come from our love and caring of people. It's truly a caring and sharing business. As we all know, people want to be in business with people they know, like and trust. Before presenting products or an opportunity, connecting is key, and building a relationship of trust is important. Sadly, many forget that it's a relationship business FIRST. Before taking the time to share about the products or business, connecting with the prospect comes first – finding out what's important to them and asking a lot of questions to see if it's even a fit before taking the next step.

It's always our intention to be of the greatest service to prospects, our community and to the company. We both subscribe to and teach the core principles of Servant Leadership which are: listening, empathy, stewardship, authenticity, compassion, honesty, open-mindedness, creating a culture of trust, patience, self-awareness and helping our team grow into their potential. We constantly strive to model and embody these characteristics for our teams, and we are grateful when we see our teammates also embody these core values.

Another key to our success is that we both love community -- creating a safe and loving community for everyone to be involved in, no matter what their level of success, experience or background. We want people to feel that they belong to something bigger than themselves and have a place to be even more of themselves as they stretch and grow.

People join a company for one of three reasons: the product, the opportunity or the community. Then, hopefully, they fall in love with the other two. In order to create community within our teams, we provide opportunities for our team to get to know each other, connecting and interacting on many different types of calls and zooms and whenever possible, providing opportunities to recognize and highlight people's success. Of course, recognition for rank advancement is important and each week we publicly acknowledge those who have reached certain levels. Also, we believe it's important to give attention to those who have other kinds of contributions, whether it's a social media admin or someone accomplished in a particular area like enrolling and retaining customers. We like to highlight them to our community on webinars.

Our team has weekly community calls, trainings and opportunity and education events, along with a newsletter to easily inform and educate. Making resources accessible and providing lots of ways to make business easier is much appreciated by our team. With training being so important, our team has a simple-to-use training website filled with an abundance of information and education. People can learn to their heart's content in one place. Getting to know the strengths and expertise of our people is a constant learning process as the team grows.

Because this business is a lifestyle business, we try to model for our teams the freedom that is available to everyone. We share our lifestyle openly, whether it's taking time off during the week to have a wonderful adventure, time with family, birthdays or learning something new… and our team appreciates getting to know us and see that they, too, can create the lifestyle of their dreams.

Finally, we want to share that our love of people and unending curiosity has led us to learn what is important to our people. Asking, listening and being constantly curious has proved very valuable, as we always want to provide what will best support our people and community.

Our team loves that we are transparent, genuine and professional. They also appreciate that sometimes we openly share that we don't agree with others, and offer our differing opinions (which sometimes gets a chuckle). When we are on team calls and zooms, we do our best to set the stage and present things in an organized, structured but free-flowing way, while always being respectful of everyone's time and not dragging things on longer than necessary.

So now I'm going to turn things over to Gregory who is going to share 10 Master Success Tips that we have learned and taught over our combined 50+ years in MLM. Our hope is that some of them will hit the mark with you and help build your competence, confidence and success in this great profession.

10 Master MLM Success Tips (from 50+ Years of Practice)

1. KIS-KID -- Keep it Simple, Keep It Duplicatable

Like many of you, we have kids (six of them) and we love to "kiss our kids. Well, in this business, one of the important keys to success is also "KIS-KID," but that means keeping it SIMPLE and keeping it DUPLICATABLE.

Chances are that the company and business you are with probably has created simple, duplicatable tools and methods of operation that have been tried, tested and proven over time. If they do, you'd be wise to learn to use and duplicate them, and not fall into the entrepreneurial trap and think you need to "innovate."

2. Be the Messenger, Not the Message

And here's some really good news, you do not have learn and memorize everything about your company, products and compensation plan. You only need to know where that information is, and how to point to and/or deliver it to your prospects, customers and distributors.

3. Let the Tools Do the Talking

To be a good messenger, you must learn to let the tools do the talking. In the early stages of building your network marketing business, you need to become familiar with your company's primary marketing materials, websites, events and your upline leaders. These are the primary "tools" that you will use to launch and build your business. Darren Hardy, the previous publisher of *Success Magazine,* says, "If you are talking, you should be pointing to a tool."

4. Work with the Willing

Your job is not to try to convince people, but rather to give people enough information to make an informed decision. Just accept the fact that your products and business are not going to be a good fit for everyone, and don't try to convince or push people into buying or joining. We learned a long time ago that "a person convinced against their will remains the same ever still." So, if you want it more for someone than they want it for themselves, even if you do convince them to buy or join, chances are it won't last. We encourage you to have the intention of sharing enough information for prospects to make a decision that is right for them, not you. As a result, the people that do say yes to being a customer or distributor will be the willing ones you can joyfully and productively work with.

5. SW, SW, SW, SW -- Some Will, Some Won't, So What, Someone's Waiting

With the intention of finding willing people who genuinely want to become customers and distributors, don't get overly attached to the outcome of your contacting and inviting efforts. In the book, *Go For No* by Richard Fenton and Andrea Waltz, they share how important it is to accept the no's as part of the journey, and know that every no gets you one step closer to the next yes. And that is something you can be happy about and look forward to! The most successful people hear no more often than others.

6. Success Is Not Magical, It's Mathematical

Simply put, it is a numbers game. And like most people, you are probably going to get more no's than yes's. That's just the way it is. If you accept that and don't take the no's personally, you will be much happier and ultimately much more successful.

If you are serious about building and succeeding in the business you are in, it is important you establish some reasonable, measurable and achievable daily prospecting and follow-up goals. For example, one success formula that really works is called 3:3:1, which means every day you commit to:

- Reaching out to **at least 3** new prospects
- Following up with **at least 3** prospects that are in your pipeline

Getting at **least 1** new prospect to a meeting, zoom or to watch a video

Sounds easy enough, doesn't it? And it is, but honestly, it will require a level of tenacity, commitment and consistency that frankly most people are not willing to stick to and do. We know from experience that if you work the numbers, the numbers will work, and your business will grow and prosper.

If you are serious about succeeding, make the decision that your head will not hit the pillow each night until you can look yourself in the mirror and smile because you completed your daily activity goal.

7. Find the Best and They will Do the Rest

This is also sometimes called "sponsoring up," and what this is referring to is that the quality of the people you prospect and enroll is going to have a huge impact on the success and growth of your organization. Think about the huge difference it could have on your success if you sponsored an energetic, enthusiastic, well-connected, self-motivated entrepreneur versus your derelict brother-in-law that takes long breaks between jobs to enjoy his unemployment benefits. Your products might be for nearly everyone, but your business surely is not.

8. Lead with the Product, Most of the Time

Many of the most successful distributors in network marketing (like us) started as customers, fell in love with the products, started sharing, and the rest, as they say, is history. Like a good book, movie or restaurant that we all lovingly and enthusiastically share with friends and family, if you believe in your product or service and radiate that belief from your heart, people will sense it and will be more likely to open up and want to learn more, or maybe even try it.

The reason we say "lead with the product, most of the time" is because usually for every three to five people that your product might be attractive and interesting to, chances are only one of them also would have responded well if you led with the business opportunity first. Even the most successful business people and best networkers know how foundational a great product or service is to a solid, long-term business opportunity. So by leading with the product, you won't alienate anyone, and it's a lot easier to open the door of discussing the opportunity after a solid appreciation for the product is established.

9. The Fortune and The Friendship Are in the Follow-Up

You'd be wise to remember this important fact of human nature: People won't care how much you know until they know how much you care. When you begin the follow-up process with your prospects, we recommend you do so with the intention of giving them enough information to make the right decision for them, not you. Begin by asking them if they have any questions, then listen carefully with the intention of understanding, not responding. The clearer you get on their personal and family situation and circumstances, the better chance you have of helping them determine if your products, services and business are a fit for them.

10. Develop Long-Term, Mutually Rewarding Relationships

This last tip we are going to leave you with is without a doubt the most important one of them all, and will be the logical and organic result of practicing the other nine we've shared with you. Network marketing is often referred to as "relationship marketing" for good reason. Regardless of the product or service you are providing, you are really in the people business.

In traditional sales, salespeople make presentations with the intention of closing a sale and earning a commission, then moving on to the next prospect.

Network marketing is similar, but actually quite different. In network marketing, we also make presentations but the intention is to open a long-term, mutually rewarding relationship that could last for years and possibly decades to come, with each customer and distributor that joins your team.

In conclusion, we feel blessed to be able to teach and model the gifts and virtues of this great profession, and our hope is to help other people to learn and do the same. What a joy it is to help people develop a dream-lifestyle while creating a residual income and being of service to others.

So bottom line, We Grow People!

Gregory and Robin Blanc Mascari

Network Marketing Professionals

For more than thirty years, Gregory has risen from the trenches to the boardroom in network marketing—building companies and organizations totaling over a million representatives and over a billion dollars in global sales.

Robin has 20+ successful years full time in network marketing with prior background in corporate leadership development as a trainer, coach and trainer of trainers.

Their love for people, devotion to timeless success and relationship principles, and ability to relate to the novice as well as the seasoned professional have been instrumental in their success and ability to develop loyal and devoted cultures and community within the field.

MARK AND JEANINE McCOOL

"You can tell what people think is important by the attention they give it."

MARK AND JEANINE McCOOL

We never intended to run a Network Marketing company. In the beginning of our story, we were like most typical American families in the '90s. I met my wife, Jeanine, while attending the University of Wisconsin. We married when we were in our early 20s, had our 3 kids in 5 years, and we both worked for several employers in those early years. We were fortunate to have family nearby to help with the kids while we both worked away from home, and even still we were just making enough money to get by.

I wasn't sure exactly what I wanted to do long-term, but I knew that I wanted to be my own boss. When I came to the end of my college experience, I was determined to put my computer science education to good use. Foreseeing a trend in information technology, I opened my own computer business in the early 1990s. Back then, there was no Best Buy or Office Max from which you could purchase a PC, and very few people were using the Internet. I could see that personal computers and Internet commerce were going to be the wave of the future. I enjoyed the computer business, but if I was not delivering a personal computer, I was not making money.

Jeanine and I were approached a few times and presented with different networking marketing opportunities, but they never seemed to be the right fit for us. One time, we were at church standing in the lobby right after service and the father of a friend ours asked us if we wanted to join them for dinner, we said sure! Then he said, "great, we will be over at 7pm tomorrow night". Jeanine and I realized too late that he had just invited himself and his wife over to our house for dinner. They did come over and the four of us sat in our family room to "fellowship". It wasn't long before he asked if we could all move to the dining room table, as it would be "more comfortable". I thought to myself, "how does it get more comfortable than sitting on our new couch"? To be accommodating and hospitable, we went to the dining room. Then, it was like a magic trick. He pulled a yellow pad of paper out of thin air and starting drawing circles and telling us about how we could join this company and share it with others to make residual income. HE SAID ALL OUR DREAMS WOULD COME TRUE!

I remember looking around at the new furniture in the brand-new home we had just built, and thought about our new Cadillac in the garage and thinking "we are not doing too badly now, what do I need this for"? You see, we were "successful" to the outside world, but we were on the treadmill of life. We were both working very hard and not being together enough as a family. They were offering us a residual opportunity; sell it once and keep earning for many years after. This was appealing, but we thought, "if we have to trick people to come over to our house in order to sign them up, this is not for us". We bought the kit for $50, put it in the closet and forgot about it.

Not too long after, we were approached by a man we had met years earlier that was coming to town. I reluctantly went to his meeting and was presented a network marketing business. Travel the world at a discount, share it with others and make money. WOW, this was right up my alley. We loved to travel, and this was so easy to share. I joined right away and started sharing it with everyone I knew. It was not long, and we could not keep up with the demand. The business was exploding, and I didn't even really know what I was doing yet. It was like a dream. Jeanine was not a big fan of the business at that time, but she was now able to stay home with the kids as I spent most of my time on the road building the business.

The leadership of the company were intrigued with the quick success that I had experienced and wanted to learn more. They called me one day out of the blue and sent me a first-class plane ticket to the corporate office. I was blown away. I couldn't believe that somebody wanted to learn from me. This was very exciting, but also a little intimidating. The meeting went very well and what was supposed to be a three-day trip turned into three weeks of collaboration.

I am a firm believer that when you are "in the race", you need to keep your blinders on, and that is what I did with this company for 2 ½ years. I refused to look at any other business or opportunity. As long as what I was doing was working, why get distracted with anything else? I just wish more people would do the same. Perseverance is the name of the game.

The time eventually came to make a change. After evaluating the marketplace and exploring two other multilevel marketing companies, from which I learned so much about what to do and what not to do, it became apparent that I was heading toward corporate ownership. While this may not have been in our plans, it was happening, and more quickly than we realized.

In 1998, a friend I had met previously called me to talk about a new company that was starting. It was in a sector that I had previously had a lot of experience. The founders wanted me to come to Florida to take a look at it, based on my previous success. It was winter in Wisconsin, and a free trip to a vacation paradise sounded nice, so I decided to go.

After meeting with the ownership team and collaborating on ideas, I secured a contract with the newly formed company. We were constantly innovating online technology for the direct sales space. Once the company began developing the tools, I started the work. Anticipation was building for this great new program, and many people were excited. However, six months into the project, it became apparent to me that we needed to redirect to make the dreams come true for the people that had joined. At that very moment, it hit me! I looked at my friend and said, "If is it going to be, it is up to me!". Right then and there, I decided I was going to redirect everything that I had been working on for the last six months into starting my own company. I just knew that I had to take everything that I had been working on to fulfill our promise to these people.

However, I had one important person to convince before the deal was sealed. I flew back home to Wisconsin, walked into our bedroom, and said to Jeanine, "we are going to start a traveling business and we're moving to Florida". She had no idea how serious I was. Two weeks later, I flew back to Florida to look for office space. By April 1999, we found offices in Florida and got incorporated. We were in business!

Knowing I needed to concentrate on building the company's infrastructure, Jeanine rolled up her sleeves and wore many hats. In the early days, when we were working around-the-clock, Jeanine was the office manager, accountant, and receptionist. You name it, she did it. As we grew, we brought on an accountant and other people to fill these positions.

This was a big deal! Jeanine had not been involved in any of the direct sales businesses we joined. Not even a little bit! It wasn't until this time that I really understood the deep-down resentment she had towards this business due to her upbringing. This had made things very challenging in the beginning. As Jeanine started to work in the business and meet the people, she started to really understand it better and appreciate what we were doing for people. She saw the impact we were making in people's lives first-hand.

Jeanine knows every aspect of the business now because she's been there and done it. She's also been a spiritual leader, coach, and mentor. Jeanine has been my rock and biggest supporter. I could never have done this without her support all along the way.

Working as a couple in the industry, we believe that, when given the right opportunity, ordinary people can do extraordinary things. We both have our roles, we "stay in our lanes", so to speak. Jeanine directs the company's events, and oversees the recognition and award programs, and I am the visionary. We attend most events together and collaborate on all big decisions.

"I really enjoy coaching and mentoring people," she says. "I believe true joy within a person comes from giving your life away, not from striving to keep it," Jeanine says. "It gives me goose bumps just talking about it, because Mark and I have learned from the beginning that it's not about us— it's about everybody else. And when we've focused on everyone else, the rewards have been plentiful and joyous."

What excites me and Jeanine the most is helping others live the kind of lives they want to live, on their terms. "Looking at people who have come into the business and seeing how much they have grown over the years has been a real blessing for us," Jeanine says. "When you see people get involved and achieve their dreams".

We never forget the most important mission of all: caring for others and making a difference in people's lives.

Our suggestions for success in the MLM industry are:

1. No matter what happens, don't give up. From the very beginning of my (Mark's) getting involved in Network Marketing, I saw the benefits and values. Even though my journey was not a straight line and I have been in more than one company, the time and financial freedom opportunity that I saw in the beginning has become true for me.

2. As a couple; respect each other's gifts and talents. Learn when to come together and when to stay in our own lanes.

3. Don't be afraid to shoot high. Surround yourself and learn from people in this industry that have achieved what you want. Brave up and reach out to those #1 income earners and ask for a conversation.

Mark & Jeanine McCool have been innovators who envision the hot products of the future, and leaders who pioneered online Direct Sales in the '90s. They are the masterminds behind some of the most unique and best-selling wellness products worldwide. Those 200+ wellness products have done over one billion dollars in sales. Mark was instrumental in growing his last venture from $284 Million a year to over $1.2 Billion in just a few years.

Mark continues to train and has speaking engagements all around the world, specializing in marketing and IT consulting. Jeanine is also a talented speaker and artist. She was recognized as a "Woman on the Move" in *Godly Business Woman* magazine. Both are very active and love to ski and play pickle ball. Jeanine is in the gym every morning and especially loves spin class.

Mark & Jeanine live in Sarasota, Florida. They have been there for 22 years and love it! They have 3 adult children and 5 granddaughters.

The commitment to giving back is woven deeply into their fabric. Their huge success in business has allowed them to make charitable efforts and donations of well over $1 Million dollars to many organizations around the globe including World Vision, Red Cross and the Special Olympics.

No matter what happens,

don't give up.

KEN AND MICHELLE ROLFSNESS

"No act of kindness, no matter how small, is ever wasted."

KEN AND MICHELLE ROLFSNESS

I am half Samoan, half Norwegian, and grew up poor in Blue Springs, Missouri. My mum was a factory worker and my dad was a janitor. There were times when seventeen family members were living together in a three-bedroom house. At times, we lived in a trailer park, just trying to make ends meet.

When I was nineteen, I served a two-year Christian mission in Brisbane, Australia and it was there I met Michelle Holzworth, whose family were well educated and very successful. A few months after my return home to America, Michelle flew here, we fell in love and a short time later got married. We had a big Samoan wedding with twelve attendants each, a twenty-four-tier cake, the works! Everyone must have thought we were very successful. However, the reality was this; I took my wife on our honeymoon to the exotic location of ... Interstate Inn. It was the cheapest place around, it was five minutes down the road, and it was $12.50 a night. That was the reality of our life.

I became a factory worker in Springdale, Arkansas and began re-treading truck tires making $5.00 an hour. It was a horrible, dingy, stinky job. If you'd come to our home, the smell of rubber dust was in air and in the furniture, along with steel shavings! It wasn't the greatest experience, but I just didn't know any better.

Long story short, Michelle's parents flew us over to Brisbane, where we ended up living with them for five years. I was back in the tire re-treading business, this time in Australia. Even though I made it into management, all that did was change the color of my shirt and put me on a salary. Basically, I made less per hour than the factory floor workers.

Something had to change! I was thirty-one years old, living with my wife's parents, and had no money in the bank. I felt I wasn't providing for Michelle as a husband should. So, I found a job working for a gentleman named Phil. Now Phil is a cool guy. In fact, he was considered one of the best businessmen in the world and was included in the "Who's Who of Business" in both 1998 and 2001. It seemed that everything Phil touched turned to gold! When I started working for him, I thought that maybe he could teach me some things. Long story short, I couldn't sell something I wasn't passionate about, AND I found out that I was about to be fired.

I had never been fired from any job before.

It was around that time that someone from church called and introduced me to the profession of Multilevel Marketing. At first, I just laughed and said thanks, but no thanks. However, I really didn't know what I was saying "no" to. Eventually, an audiotape was sent to me and I listened to it. Thinking this could be something good, I borrowed the money and got involved with the company.

Michelle was very upset and said there was no way we were doing that type of business, but I just knew I was tired of working in the factory, tired of living with her parents, and I needed to do something different.

So, I went to Phil and asked him to listen to that audiotape. I said to him: "you're rich and I'm poor; tell me what you think." Phil was so impressed with what he heard, he and his wife flew business class to America to see if this was the real deal. They met the owners of the company, and they liked what they saw.

Upon their return, Phil called me and asked for my business ID number. When I asked why, Phil said "well, you introduced me to this company, and I'd like to get started." I thought, WOW! This Amazing and Successful businessman and I are going to work together!

It was June 3rd, 1998 and by September, just a few months later, I walked into Phil's office and showed him my check. I said here's my part-time pay, working about fifteen hours a week compared to your full-time pay to me, working sixty to eighty hours a week. I told him I could no longer afford to work for him and that HE was fired! The cool thing about all this is, just a few months later, Phil sold that particular business and began working with me full-time. In fact, he and I have been around the world many times together. It's been really exciting because, since 1998, Michelle and I have also been around the world, dozens of times.

Regarding having success in the Network Marketing industry, here are some tips from what I have learned:

Don't judge a book by its cover. I was THAT person. I was dead set against the MLM industry, so much so that I would even sabotage people trying to share their business. Look at me now! I love this industry, am a top income earner, and it has changed my life for the better.

You never know what is in someone's heart. I always lead with the business. Most people don't know that they need your product, and at the same time, most people know they need more money. Remember that the average person needs 5-12 exposures to make a commitment to join. Find a way to make it happen, and then help them get their investment back as soon as possible.

My biggest success tool is this: I was told early on in my career that if I could get 5 people to answer my call to action (listen to my audiotape), only 1 would take action and become a customer or a team member. As a result, EVERY WEEK, for 5 out of 7 days, I would not go to bed until I had that tape in the hands of 5 people. One of my famous sayings to them was "If you can press <PLAY>, you can make money". Because I did that single, dedicated activity for three months, I was rewarded with that large check which allowed me to "fire my boss". I haven't looked back.

The profession of Multilevel Marketing has been extremely gratifying as I am so fortunate to serve and help others. I will also add that one year after starting my MLM career, I was able to save enough money to buy Michelle a seven-bedroom resort-style dream home, and life with her continues to be wonderful!

Ken & Michelle Rolfsness have been married since 1988 and love spending time with each other, especially having lazy days on the beaches of the world. They have 3 amazing children, Rebecca, Jackson, and Zachary. All three are young adults, successful and leaders in their own fields, as well as gifted musicians. Michelle is a Director in the early childhood education field, where she passionately advocates daily for the empowerment of children and their human rights. Ken has been a professional drummer for decades and performs all over the world!

Ken & Michelle are Authors, Speakers, Network Marketing Professionals, Entrepreneurs, and Community Heroes. They serve on several Boards and committees and their whole family volunteers heavily in St George, Utah where they currently live.

Don't judge a book by its cover.
You never know what is in
someone's heart.

ROBIN YOUNGE AND SARAH LOVELY

"We believe in turning intentions into done"

ROBIN YOUNGE AND SARAH LOVELY

Here we are again. Going to the grocery store to get appetizers and drinks for the in-home meeting that would take place in our house. It seems like this happens almost every weekend. We always played the same roles. I would help set the house up, move the computer from one room to the main room, put the food, and drinks out, and rearrange the couch and chairs to accommodate the handfuls of people who were about to walk through the door. As everyone started to arrive, I would go downstairs with the dogs, and binge watch whatever show was on my list at the time, leaving Sarah to work her magic upstairs.

Once I would hear the shuffling of footsteps getting closer to the door, I would pop upstairs, say goodbye as they were putting on their coats and shuffling around to find the other shoe that seemed to be misplaced from the pile. All the while being glad that another evening was done. Most of the time we would just go to bed, and we would clean the next morning. As I looked around at empty glasses, paper plates, and our computer left in the living room for the presentation, I didn't understand why Sarah kept doing this.

Sarah fell in love with the idea of being an entrepreneur long before we ever met. On an average day doing average things being a Mum, she stumbled upon her local newspaper about a stay-at-home Mom who was building a business from home. After reading the article, Sarah knew without a doubt this was her journey. Something sparked within her. That inner voice within was begging to be let out. An adventure was begging for the attempt to be free. Not having traditional schooling, she felt a lack of personal purpose, and wondered if success as a contributor financially was in her future. After reading that someone just like her was succeeding, Sarah knew this was something she could not let go. It was time to delve into more. As a Mumma, all that came with this adventure hit home. Build a business from anywhere. Create your own hours. Meet new people. Guide people to become better versions of themselves. Everything hit the mark.

On the other hand, I was a little slow to the party. While Sarah was designing her own life, I was focusing my energy on building my musical career. This was a rigorous journey with very little payout. It is all well to be driven by passion, but there comes a time when one yearns for a deeper sense of significance.

After watching and supporting Sarah through her journey as an entrepreneur, or shall I say a designer of life on her own terms, I decided I wanted a little piece of the action.

Now I want to make this absolutely clear! Sarah was absolutely crushing her business! Sarah was serious. She made plans. She had purpose. Sarah took the entire family on an unforgettable family trip to Hawaii, all from the income of her business.

Here's what most people don't understand about Network Marketing. The level of success one has is in direct proportion to the level of success you help guide others to have. This is what makes our model one of the best in the world to help create, not just financial opportunity, but a better person. When someone levels up, and earns more, becomes more, they in turn help those surrounding them do just the same.

This is where I directly came in. After watching the woman I love become more driven, financially earning more, investing in herself, the more I found myself wanting to be a part of this with her. The attractive qualities of what this model brought I didn't want to leave on the table. The potential was just too high. I, as well, had no traditional schooling outside of high school. I barely even made it out alive! When I would look at successful people, I felt stuck. I felt like success was not in the cards for me. What was I going to do? I wasn't going to go back to school. There wasn't anything in the slightest I was interested in doing that warranted going into debt with a student loan.

Let's jump ahead many moons into the second part of this chapter.

It's been 5 years now that we have stepped into the arena of working together full time in building our business. We've travelled together, won awards together, walked across stages together, changed companies together, and most importantly our relationship has grown even stronger together.

You see, we both came from a similar place where we knew there were better versions of us within ourselves. We both knew we wanted more for ourselves. This made us a powerful duo, taking on the ups and downs of building a business from the ground up.

But here's the deal. Building any professional business as a power couple comes with its challenges, both together, and separately. We've had to learn to become each other's best friend, and biggest fan along the way in order to make this work. We've had to make temporary sacrifices with our kids, travel at times to support the team, and hire someone to watch our pups and cats at home. For us, as huge animal lovers, that left us feeling homesick weeks before travelling anywhere. We both are the all-in type people. If we commit, we've committed.

No matter what company an individual chooses to align with, a level of professionalism is always required. This is why we are always upping our game when it comes to education, leadership, and strategies, so we can be ever evolving into the best versions of ourselves. In order for us to help more, we know we have to become more.

In the 21st century more and more people are choosing to spend more time doing what they love with those they love. Less people are choosing to work somewhere else away from home.

In fact, people are choosing to earn less to be with those they love, more often than not, while also doing more of what they want.

We know just how powerful this model is for those who choose to adopt their entrepreneurial spirit into themselves. To say YES to what could be.

All one has to do is show up to the possibility of more, and we can help guide them along the journey just as others have for us.

Where else can you enter an arena, play at whatever level you choose, and still be accepted by the masses? Full time, part time, limited time or no availability at all, and still be accepted.

Many positive actions have taken place in building our business, but there have also been a few that have required the largest level of growth from us. Sarah and I always want the best for people, and at times that has been to our detriment. We've had to come to learn that our role is to help guide people to building their own business, but we will not build it for them. That was a major lesson for us. Allowing people to play at whatever level they choose to, no matter what we see their abilities to be. People need time to blossom. I know that one firsthand. It took both of us years to see what was right in front of us as possibilities, and, to this day, we are continually evolving into more.

So, what are the stories you're telling yourself? Do you wish you had something in your life that brought greater fulfillment? Maybe something that brought excitement? Perhaps you're looking for an environment of people who would believe in you, and the untapped potential you feel stirring within yourself just wishing to be set free?

A bird once sang that the purpose of life is to be all you can be with all you've been given.

As Sarah and I look back at where we were before we decided to take this journey, we both realize why we didn't do more, earlier. The only reason we didn't show up to more potential sooner, and over the years of meeting people it tends to be the same conclusion for most folks, Fear!

No matter where you are, and what you're doing just know this: It's not supposed to be without fear. The fear you feel within yourself of doubt, time, reasoning, education, support, or whatever story that's circling around your mind, fear only shows itself when the potential of growth shows up at your doorstep. The rational mind will do its job to rationalize why you should stay safe, but if you look at fear from the other side of the curtain you will see that fear is a gift letting you know potential is knocking. That the unknown is waiting. It's one of the greatest gifts of this model. A community of people all working through similar situations. I don't know of another area where we all get to come together to be paid to level up.

Friedrich Nietzsche once said, "Whoever has a why to live can bear almost any how".

We feel honoured that you've taken the time to get to know us just a little bit during this brief interaction and appreciate the opportunity of being with you. We hope we offered just a little spark into who you could become, and the powerful environment Network Marketing could add to your life.

We leave you with this. Which would you regret more? The pain of discipline or the pain of regret?

With much love, and success,

Sarah & Robin.

Bio:

Sarah Lovely & Robin Younge

Hey Friends, we are excited that you are here with us!

We are Sarah and Robin. We live in beautiful Vancouver, Canada. We have 2 cats, 2 dogs, and 3 kids. We spend most of our days being Social Marketers, exercising, and spending time with our family. Laughing is something you'll hear coming from our house all day.

We believe in 'turning intentions into done'.

What does that mean?

As humans, we tend to create a version of ourselves in our mind that seldom ever sees the light of day. Whether that be a better body, better parents, greater friends, abundance in finances, or just an overall sense of well-being. We understand that if we could just be 1% better today than yesterday, that we could build a foundation of belief we could then add to.

Another deep passion of ours is helping people who want a greater financial future to be surrounded by our like-minded passion-filled community. This is an important step. Community!

We believe that sometimes we just need a mentor in our corner who believes in us. Someone who is there by our side helping us along the journey of what's unknown, so we can become that version of ourselves that we know deep down we are meant to become!

To your health & wealth,

Much love,

Sarah & Robin

The purpose of life

is to be all you can be

with all you've been given.

BRENDA LEE AND JIM GALLATIN

"For I know the plans I have for you, declares the Lord, plans to prosper you and not to harm you, plans to give you hope and a future."

Jeremiah 29:11

BRENDA LEE AND JIM GALLATIN

When I was asked to be a contributor for this project and share my experience and my wisdom in this world of entrepreneurism, and particularly in this industry of Network Marketing as a couple, my first knee jerk thought was WHAT????

You see my beloved and cherished life partner, business partner, best friend forever and always 'til death do we part, has gone on to heaven ahead of me. He said he felt he was slipping away and that he would go on and find us a "good spot!" ... of course, a gorgeous beach spot! That's a typical state for him ... a little shot of humor when he wasn't even trying, and always, *always* wanting to love, protect, and provide.

In honor of him, my Honey Jim, I will share with you how we did this Network Marketing thing together.

I could have never anticipated the life journey I was about to embark on when I said yes to a blind date and got into that beautiful blue and white '54 Buick. Nor did he have a clue of the fiery, spirited young filly he would meet and spend the rest of his life with.

For sure, his patience and tolerance helped tremendously. HE KEPT ME!!!!!! He was EXCEPTIONAL, EXTRAORDINARY, LONG-SUFFERING, GOOD TO THE CORE, AND HE LOVED ME!

My introduction *into* and my love *for* the world of sales started very young. I was just six or seven when my friend Sandy and I set up a lemonade stand by our rock wall in front of our saltbox style New England home. All these years later I remember it clearly! It was a warm sunny day, the fragrant smell of freshly cut grass in the air. I smell the fragrance of lilacs wafting in the gentle breeze. There were little trails of greenery poking through the crevices of the rocks and on the dirt sidewalk. Our little card table was covered with a pretty yellow flower print cloth complemented with my Mom's lapis blue pitcher and colorful assorted cups from her FiestaWare collection. Our boisterous, colorful parrot, Polly, was in her cage just next to the front steps to the house. Mom would put her there when the weather was nice. When folks would stop by, she would get very excited and agitated and say over and over, "Doffy, Doffy, HELP!" My Mom's name was Dorothy and that was as close to her name as Polly could say. She definitely heightened people's curiosity and made for a good sales partner.

We were just two little girlfriends, giddy with excitement, waving people to stop and enjoy a refreshing lemonade. When the lemonade was all gone, we split the money and trotted straight for the Apothecary and perched right up to the soda fountain onto the spinning stools, ordered an ice cream cone, and filled our little bag with penny candy. Now that really dates me, doesn't it? How is THAT for a first successful sales experience? Who knew I was bitten with the Entrepreneur Bug way back then?

Hmmmm ... WORK = PAID. I liked it. FUN!

As a kid I was always selling something! Greeting cards, garden seed, Girl Scout cookies etc..

These INNOCENT, CHILDHOOD, SUCCESSFUL ACTIVITIES are surely some of the THREADS IN MY LIFE'S TAPESTRY.

Soon after Jim and I married, the babies started arriving lickety-split, and money was tight ... very tight! I learned that I could just "sign up" for whatever company I wanted to and get a nice discount and, holy moly, if I shared and sold some, I would get paid! Along came multiple companies through the years and from those companies I received awards, gifts, and recognition that were all incredible, and our family enjoyed them as well. If I have any regret, it is that I wish I would have seen Network Marketing as the serious profession that it is and not just to get products at a discount. I LOVE the industry of Network Marketing and I am good at it. I truly love being able to make people better through sharing the opportunity Network Marketing offers. I love the team of people we get to work with and how we become friends and family. I also love the culture of reaching up, down, across groups ... not just in our own team, but throughout the industry.

Our efforts over the years, along with the opportunity our current and forever company offers, are providing me with peace of mind and comfort as I enter into the Golden Years. It's so worth the effort. It's not an overnight success. It definitely is a real straight up business and, if you treat it like a business, it will grow and reward you well. I tell everyone that MLM Security beats Social Security any day. We have earned significant income, beautiful trips and cars etc., and the most valuable thing of all is the friendships we have made along the way.

Teammates = friendships = family :)

I love our products and I love our company, and that makes for easy sharing.

When Jim and I met, he was in the Navy. After the Navy he worked at 3M and a couple other jobs until he answered God's calling into ministry. So many wonderful memories and friends from that season of our life. The kids were tykes and, following his graduation from seminary and his ordination into ministry, he was now Pastor Jim and I was Pastor Jim's wife. I'm smiling saying that, and here is why .... Remember, I have always had a foot in network marketing and in the ensuing years, as I achieved top ranks and became known in the various companies, Jim was called Brenda Lee's husband:) So, a little roll reversal was happening depending on where we were! We laughed whenever that happened. This was another example of support for one another.

We moved our family quite a few times; from Midwest to west coast, back to Midwest, and finally settled in the west. All the while, with kids everywhere and each needing to be somewhere for school or sports etc., Jim would come home from work and pitch right in with whatever needed to be done. All the things that go along with having a big family. Farm chores, meal prep, clean up, sort products for delivery (yes, we did actually deliver to the customers back then). Thankfully, today it's all drop ship right to the door directly from the companies.

He was a genuine partner in business and was always grateful for my efforts and for our loyal, faithful customers and business partners. He was also grateful for the many glorious perks that we earned. I am indeed a blessed woman to have had such support in all my endeavors.

I went back to school after number five child and earned a Bachelor of Arts and later a Masters of Applied Behavioral Science degree. I continued my love of learning by earning many more certifications;

which have served me well, and tons and tons of life experiences; both good and ugly.

Believe me! I could write volumes if I wrote our life story, and I just may do that someday. However, to address the topic of doing this thing called Network Marketing TOGETHER while raising a family, working, and going to school etc. etc., the greatest gifts Jim gave me and our family were his steadfast and undying love, belief, encouragement, and support!!!! No matter what crazy idea or another thing I wanted to BE and DO, he always encouraged and stood by me, and told me to GO FOR IT!

He was always my greatest cheer leader.

He didn't balk at me for signing up for yet A n o t h e r T h i n g! He sure could have! I know there were times I shouldn't have spent the money! I know there were times I was gone to do another party or training etc., and he stayed with the kids and made dinner; whatever was necessary.

Along with the fantastic benefits of this industry such as: being able to sleep until you're done and setting your work schedule around YOUR life instead of you working for a boss and their schedule, there is the huge benefit of no cap or ceiling on your income. You are building to make YOUR dreams come true! Travel the world if you choose, support causes you love and believe in. Leave a legacy, and let's not forget the FUN FACTOR!

One huge heart desire was to earn enough money to take our whole family on a very special unforgettable trip, and THAT dream did come true. In the second year in my forever company, Jim and I took 34 of us on an all-expenses paid trip to Maui. It was spectacular and there were so many wonderful memories. I hired a chef and live musician to our huge suite and lanai for dinner time and, besides our beautiful three-bedroom suite, I provided seven other suites for the family. I reserved a big ol' catamaran just for our family for an unforgettable snorkeling trip and a fantastic luau. Plus, let's not forget the hours and hours spent at the beach and pools. Jim and I were overjoyed to be able to do this with our family. A huge dream was realized. By the way, there have been five additions to our family since then!

We both are made of the stuff to love people unconditionally, and our hearts' desire and intent is to Make People Better. We have loved well and worked well together for our lifetime. Jim had his own magic with people and he attracted many folks in our different endeavors along life's path. He was kind, loving, generous, encouraging, an excellent listener, genuine, wonderfully funny, and so wise. He truly did minister to many people whether it be behind the pulpit, visiting in homes and hospitals, or in his role as Police chaplain.

BIG TIP for success in life is to love one another unconditionally, without judgement. Lift each other up. Encourage each other to GO-BE-DO what they are passionate about. You never know how powerful and life-changing your words can be. Out of the same mouth come praise and cursing, and this is important to know. Words can build someone up or words can destroy. Couples working together in this industry can be a very positive force for good or just the opposite, a force for destruction, just with their words to each other. Thus, I encourage you to keep guard over your tongue. Read for yourself about the power of the tongue in the Bible; James 3:3-12. So, I say, PRAISE, PRAISE and PRAISE some more!!! You can never over praise someone! People, step up to praise! Marriages can be saved by compliments and words of praise! I feel strongly about this topic because I know firsthand when one half of a couple has a strong desire and dream to be successful in Network Marketing and the partner is opposed for various beliefs and reasons. It creates tremendous resentment and unfulfilled dreams.

Especially praise and encourage the love of your life, and certainly your kids. Thank God for them always and unconditionally.

Notice every little thing and acknowledge it with thanks! Give at least three compliments daily. Just try it for a couple weeks and notice!

I GET IT! You may not have that supportive spouse encouraging you to GO-BE-DO your passion and fulfill your dreams, and it's hard. The greatest gifts you can have from your spouse are support and encouragement. Your spouse may not want anything to do with Network Marketing and he/she may even think you are off your rocker (along with other family members) and that is perfectly ok. What they CAN do is be supportive of you and what you are doing for yourself and the family. Make money, earn a car, take him/her on that beautiful all-expense paid trip you earned! Not to rub it in, but does your spouse earn an all-expense paid trip EVERY YEAR as a reward for the many hours worked? They will come around, and love and appreciate you for all you do to enhance their life.

Now I don't want you thinking that this is just for folks who want to go to the moon or be a top-income earner. Many, *many* are just wanting or needing $500 a month to help with the mortgage or car payment or groceries or just shoe shopping! The beautiful thing about this industry is that it can be whatever you want it to be.

TIP: Find what you love! Find what makes your heart sing WITH PASSION, and what brings you joy! Find the products and the company that align with your values and integrity and don't second guess! Don't procrastinate and over think it! JUST SAY YES! Stick and stay, and never go away. Dream Big and IGNITE that Burning Desire from within! Desire deeply! Desire performs the "impossible"! Believe in yourself, have faith you can GO-BE-DO whatever your heart desires and GO FOR IT!!

TIP: Be teachable and coachable! Be plugged in to everything your company offers: trainings, classes, meetings, videos and recordings, read, read, read and read some more!

TIP: Be a student of the industry and of your company. Read Jeff Olson's book: THE SLIGHT EDGE, and then read it a couple more times. Give it to several people. It is not a how-to book just for Network Marketing, or any specific company. It is a wonderful book about slight edge activities relating to every area of your life. Every waking hour we are making some sort of decision based on our life philosophy, which is the way we think about simple everyday things. Read this simple yet profound life changing book, let it sink in, and act on what you glean from it. Allow the philosophy shared to sink in and guide you! Be a student of yourself! Personal development is worthwhile, and investing in yourself is dollars well spent.

Remember, thoughts are things and the power that signals success is the power of your mind. I am a perpetual student and I have so much more to learn! I love learning and will continue until I'm in my box! I highly recommend you do the same.

Let me close with a favorite scripture.

Jerimiah 29:11

For I know the plans I have for you, declares the Lord, plans to prosper you and not to harm you, plans to give you hope and a future.

My Honey Jim Gallatin was a good man! 1938-2021

I have been cherished!

I could never have made it this far without him!

He loved his family immeasurably, to the moon and back!

We rode a lot of water together, as Jim always used to say. How we managed to make this work as a couple was with a lot of GRACE and "Yes Dear" 😊

I am forever grateful to God for His providence and orchestrating our being together 63 years of our life. We raised six amazing kids, five sons and one daughter. They have given us 16 grandkids and 5 great grandkids (so far)!

Thanks for listening:)

Brenda Lee Gallatin MA ABS, MFC, CDC, DASA, DVIT

Mom, Nana, Great Nana! Favorite thing in whole world is when we can ALL be together:)

Lives in Lacey, Washington. Born in Beverly Farms, Massachusetts. Lived in Minnesota and Oregon too.

Entrepreneur, Author, Coach, Speaker

Loves The Lord, Bible study, loves to be with family, the beach, horses, the smell of the farm, her little dog, knitting, painting, writing, speaking, reading, theater, music, baby *anything*, travel, personal development, restaurants, farmers market .... Owner at: *I Make Life Better*

Retired Marriage and Family Therapist, specialized in domestic violence treatment as well as CDC (chemical dependency addictions).

Perpetual Network Marketing Professional!

Books IN MY LIBRARY I treasure and recommend:

Bible

The Slight Edge: Turning Simple Disciplines INTO Massive Success & Happiness by Jeff Olson

Any and ALL books by John C. Maxwell, Napoleon Hill, Wallace D. Wattles, Jim Rohn, Zig Ziglar, Bob Proctor, Tony Robbins, Shad Helmstetter, James Clear, Brian Tracy, T. Harv Eker, Eric Worre, Wayne Dyer, Stephen Covey, Dale Carnegie, Robert Kiyosaki, Simon Sinek, Jordan Adler, Hal Elrod, Jen Sincero, Darren Hardy, Richard Bliss Brooke, George S. Clason, Bob Burg, Malcolm Gladwell, Michael A. Singer

Many, many others, in a variety of genres! Did I tell you …? I LOVE BOOKS!!

You can never over praise someone!

YOU

YOU

This chapter is waiting for your name at the top. It's waiting for your quote, for your bio at the bottom of the page, for your beautiful picture where you can't help but have the biggest smile, it's waiting for your story of success. It is here as a blank page waiting for you to tell us who you are, what inspired you to "try" network marketing and how your decision for a better life has changed everything for you and the people you care for the most.

We're waiting to read on your pages what dreams you have seen realized. We are waiting to read how you jumped in right away after reading this book ... or the process you went through in deciding about joining us and how long it took you ... hours, days, or weeks to say YES.

Or, maybe you're already in Network Marketing, and this chapter is here waiting for you. After reading this book, you understood in your heart and in your mind that IT'S TIME for you to take your business seriously. It's time to move it into a place where it serves you in relationship to those very dreams and needs you have that cross your mind each night, and that are in your prayers each morning. These are the things you talk about to your friends and family that you really want to have "one day".

Maybe this chapter is being left for your journey, your experiences, your struggles, your aspirations, and your path to freedom: whatever that means to you.

These pages await your untold story. You will share how you were able to help yourself, your family, your friends, or your community because, ONE DAY, you decided that if all these people in this book could do it, SO COULD YOU!

Maybe this chapter is where you are going to write your advice to the next person you want this industry to bless. Maybe this is where you'll share what helped you break through your limiting beliefs, or the secrets of hope that got you past your fears. Perhaps you'll share that, when you finally said that deep-seated yes *inside,* everything in your life got better -- even before the financial rewards came to you. You realized when you finally made a decision in the right direction and just did the simple act of saying yes and having faith, a door was opened: the door to the part of you that believes in unlimited possibilities. That simple act alone has made the relationships in your life today 100 percent better, you smile more, you walk differently, you feel lighter, and everyone notices that something is different about you.

This chapter is being held FOR YOU. We care about YOU.

THIS BOOK was written for YOU. THESE STORIES were shared for YOU.

Let us be the first to say CONGRATULATIONS! These pages are waiting for YOUR words and we all can't wait to read them VERY SOON.

It's time for YOUR CHAPTER.

THANK YOU

I want to share my gratitude to these generous authors. They exemplify the very values upon which this industry has been built. Network Marketing is unique for many different reasons, the freedom of time, the ability to have the income one chooses, support from people that you may never have met before, the camaraderie, the incredible expansion of your personal development, and the opportunity to build a legacy.

I want to personally thank all the authors and contributors to this book.

These authors have just gone above and beyond to share not only their stories for us to relate to and be inspired by but in these stories are the lessons that they have learned that helped propel them to the success and happiness they have today and for that I am grateful. If you are reading this book and already in this incredible profession, I tip my hat to you and encourage you to stick and stay until those dreams of yours start to unfold. If you are not in this profession and have read this book and think you have heard something that makes you want to know more or your gut is saying this is precisely what you're looking for then act on those feelings and take the next step to learn more.

It has been an incredible pleasure to get to know each and every one of these authors, once again you are amazing and I appreciate the time and energy that you put into this incredible book for not only our profession but for the many people that will step into this profession in the future and have their lives changed.

ABOUT DEB DRUMMOND

Deb Drummond lives in beautiful Vancouver, Canada. She is the mother of her two favourite people: her daughter, Chloae, and her son, Ocean. With her new title of YaYa, she gets to add to that "favourite list" Brynlee and Kashton.

Deb is a pioneer in the world of entrepreneurship. As a visionary, she was one of the first in her country to create companies in the health and wellness sector. To date, she has created 7 companies and inspired thousands around the globe.

She is an award-winning business owner, with achievements that have never been done before. She is a leader in opening local and international markets.

Deb's thirty-year deep dive of study and training in Top Performance has built her reputation in the field as a speaker, mastermind trainer and personal coach. She has inspired, educated, and motivated audiences of over 20 thousand to stand to their feet. In her private practice, Deb has personally worked with over 30 thousand clients, moving them to a higher state of optimal health and wealth.

A well-known radio host of the Mission Accepted podcast, Deb interviews dynamic Entrepreneurs, Ultrapreneurs, Creatives, and Media Professionals who reveal personal life stories and secrets to the success of 'making it' in the world of entrepreneurship. Deb is the founder of Mission Accepted Media where she creates anthologies and books about people and business. She is the creator of the ever so popular Top Performance Day Planner and Tracker.

Deb loves music and is happiest when she is connecting people that she knows will benefit from meeting each other and, if you were to go to her home, you would be greeted with a table of "treats" that look like she took over Willy Wonka's candy shop!

www.DebDrummond.com

ABOUT MISSION ACCEPTED MEDIA

The name Mission Accepted took a lot of time to polish. It was essential to have a name that truly represented what needs to take place, both fundamentally and at the core of every person who decides to become a self-starter.

Entrepreneurship on every level captures the essence of anyone willing to take "on the mission" of creating a life by design. Whether it's the singer that is looking for their big break, the entrepreneur looking to make their mark in the marketplace, the actor waiting to be discovered, or the radio host who is building an audience, if you said" yes" to making your own way in your career, then you took on "the mission".

Before one says yes to being an entrepreneur, there most likely have been a lot of conversations going on with other people, advisors, and close friends, and for sure in the confines of one's own mind. One must make the decision to say yes on the inside: in your heart, your brain, or both before the word YES comes out of your mouth and the excitement starts! We understand those moments so well!!

We wanted to create many platforms to offer what entrepreneurs need the most: the right kind of exposure. We wanted to celebrate that spirit of YES by assisting and creating an easier way to do that. Deborah Drummond, the owner of Mission Accepted, has been an entrepreneur for close to 30 years and knows firsthand the behind-the-scenes work it takes to make it. It was her vision to offer a plethora of support through media opportunities to help current and future entrepreneurs have smoother, easier, and faster success.

Deb was a pioneer in entrepreneurship, building her legacy before we had smartphones and social media. She understands the challenges that can be brought to all generations who want to "make their own mark " and her goal is to create a safe, successful place for all generations, even these new incredible gen Z's, to land.

Mission Accepted Media is made available to anyone needing a place to get the word out about who they are, what they do, and what they need. It is also a place for everyone, entrepreneurs or not, to come and be inspired by the stories, the climb, the diversity, and the unbelievable creativity that these crazy folks draw from to keep on keeping on.

Mission Accepted Media hosts an incredible podcast, including live podcasts on stage at events, or in the comforts of your home studio, aka your desk! We also publish collaboration anthologies of incredible books that encourage the rise and celebration of entrepreneurship.

Mission Accepted Media recognizes entrepreneurship shows up in many different ways which is why we highlight Entrepreneurs, Ultrapreneurs, Creatives such as artists, singers, actors, and authors as well as self-started Media like radio, podcasts, tv hosts, and print publications.

Please reach out to explore opportunities to be on the show, as well if you'd like to be featured in one of the books or if you have an event and want live podcasts on-site.

May you keep your Mission alive, whatever that means to you!

Passion is the fuel to expansion and expansion is one of life's best gifts!

In good health and new friendships,

Deb Drummond

OTHER PUBLICATIONS

Top Performance Success Tracker
This is ultimate system for keeping track of all your contacts and follow-up steps. Designed and used by Deb Drummond.

Top Performance Success Planner
Designed to complement your Success Tracker, Deb has created a full-year day planning system, embedded with inspirational quotes from top leaders around the globe.

Mission Accepted: 262 Women Entrepreneurs, Ultrapreneurs, Creatives and Media Rock Legacy and Tell All
The largest inspired collection of life wisdom in a beautifully designed coffee-table book.

Entrepreneurial Women over 50 Rocking Social Media
An incredible collection of stories of businesswomen who were faced with having to relearn a new way of doing business. This is a how-to that was learned because it was a have-to.

Manufactured by Amazon.ca
Bolton, ON